D1600834

MARQUETTE
UNIVERSITY

PRESS

REFORMATION TEXTS
WITH TRANSLATION (1350–1650)

Kenneth Hagen, General Editor

Series: **Biblical Studies**
Franz Posset, Editor

Volume 3

MARQUETTE
UNIVERSITY

PRESS
MILWAUKEE, 1998

The *POSTILLA*
of NICHOLAS OF LYRA
on the SONG OF SONGS

Introduced, Translated, and Edited
by James George Kiecker

MARQUETTE UNIVERSITY PRESS
MILWAUKEE

The Association of Jesuit University Presses

Cataloguing-in-Publication Data

Nicholas, of Lyra, ca. 1270-1349.
　　[Postilla super Cantica. English & Latin]
　　The Postilla of Nicholas of Lyra on the Song of Songs /
introduced, translated, and edited by James George Kiecker.
　　p. cm. — (Reformation texts with translation (1350-1650).
Biblical studies ; v. 4)
　　English and Latin on facing pages.
　　Includes bibliographical references (p. 24).
　　ISBN 0874627036
　　1. Bible. O.T. Song of Solomon—Commentaries—Early works to
1800. I. Kiecker, James George. II. Title. III. Series.
　　BS1485.3 .N5313 1998
　　223'.907—ddc21
　　　　　　　　　　　　　　　　　　　　　　　　　　　98-8884
　　　　　　　　　　　　　　　　　　　　　　　　　　　CIP

Printed in the United States of America

© Marquette University Press, 1998

Dedicated to
my wife, Susan,
in token of her support

CONTENTS

FOREWORD

Reformation Texts With Translation (1350-1650) (RTT) are published by Marquette University Press, Andrew Tallon, Director. RTT are brief theological and religious works from the fourteenth through the seventeenth centuries translated into English usually for the first time.

The purpose is to provide religious works that are not easily available to those students of this period in need of primary sources and in need of maintaining the languages. We thereby seek to keep alive the tradition of *textus minores*. The criteria for the selection of texts will be solid, intellectual, and exciting material that will entice our students to dig deeper into the primary languages from the Renaissance and Reformation.

The texts are aimed at a wide audience of scholars, students, persons working in religious areas (such as churches or synagogues), as well as at laymen and laywomen interested in pursuing religious readings from the Renaissance. To facilitate their use, each text features the original language and English translation on facing pages.

Latin and German were our first languages; thereafter, we will include texts in Dutch, French, and Spanish. Since the goal is not only to make more works (from 1350 to 1650) available in translation but also to encourage scholars to continue in original language study, we first selected works done in manageable Latin.

Three series within RTT are currently in production: Biblical Studies, edited by Dr. Franz Posset; Women of the Reformation, edited by Prof. Merry Wiesner-Hanks; and the Late Reformation, edited by Prof. Robert Kolb.

Kenneth Hagen
General Editor

PREFACE

In an age when doctors of the Church were given distinctive titles, Nicholas of Lyra's title was the *Doctor planus et utilis,* "the clear and useful doctor." It was a fitting sobriquet. The scholar, the preacher, the friar often sought a handy, up-to-date reference book to unlock the meaning of a scriptural passage. And there, from the early fourteenth to the late seventeenth century, were the commentaries of Nicholas of Lyra. Verse by verse, scholarly yet employing simple Latin, offering alternate translations, always going out of his way to be understood, Lyra tried to be of service to his readers. *Planus et utilis* indeed!

Today Lyra is largely unknown. But things may be changing. A new generation of scholars is showing interest in medieval biblical commentaries, often assessing their impact on Reformation thinking and writing. Such individuals should find the present volume helpful. Besides this, the sheer fact that this volume makes available a medieval Latin text with accompanying translation may arouse the interest of scholars, students, and a general audience in this area of medieval studies, as well as in Lyra specifically. This is our hope.

No scholarly work is the achievement of a single person. Rather, it depends on the help and encouragement of others. No one feels this more acutely than this translator. He must thank Dr. Franz Posset, Prof. John Patrick Donnelly, S.J., and especially Prof. Kenneth Hagen of Marquette University. Their efforts improved the translation immensely. In this new age of computers, no small thanks must also go to the manuscript's principal typist, Mrs. Diane Koser of Wisconsin Lutheran College. The aim of the translator was to be, like Lyra, "clear and useful," and he takes responsibility for all failings.

James George Kiecker
Milwaukee, 1997

INTRODUCTION

I. Lyra's Life

Not much is known about the life of Nicholas of Lyra. The reader is directed to the sources listed in the Selected Bibliography. He was probably born about 1270 in Neuve-Lyre near Évreux on the coast of Normandy. To account for his later knowledge of Hebrew it has been suggested that he was wholly or partly Jewish. But he may simply have studied at Hebrew schools in Évreux, a center of Jewish biblical exegesis in the thirteenth century. Quite clearly he was influenced by Rabbi Solomon ben Isaac (1030-1105), better known as Rashi, whom he quotes frequently.

In 1300 or 1301 (or perhaps already in 1291 or 1292), Lyra joined the Order of Friars Minor. He became a master of theology in 1308, and by 1309 he had an established position on the theological faculty at Paris. He also rose quickly to high administrative positions in his order, becoming provincial of several French provinces. In 1322 he sided with those Franciscans who believed the order should own no property (the Spirituals) rather than those who believed the order could (the Conventuals). He seems to have resigned from his administrative duties in 1330 to devote more time to study.

Lyra's writings met with immediate success. There is no evidence of controversy surrounding Lyra or opposition to his writing during his lifetime. However, in 1429, about eighty years after his death, a converted Jew and Spanish bishop, Paul of Burgos (ca. 1350-1435), published a work criticizing Lyra for not following the commentaries of the fathers, for being unskilled in Hebrew, and for relying too much on Rashi. Subsequently, a German Franciscan, Matthias Döring (ca. 1400-1469), wrote a stern defense of Lyra against Burgos. Döring in turn was criticized by the Dominican Archbishop of Seville, Diego Deza (ca. 1444-1523), who felt that Döring in his reply to Burgos had been unjust to Thomas Aquinas. With this the controversy over scriptural interpretation became principally theological, and came to an end.

There has been some discussion about the date of Lyra's death. Lyra's tomb was apparently in the chapter hall of the convent of the Cordeliers in Paris. An epitaph in verse, placed there at an unknown date, stated that he died on October 23, 1340. The tomb was seriously damaged by fire in November of 1580, and this epitaph was destroyed. The tomb was restored in 1631, and an epitaph in prose was placed on it. This epitaph has also disappeared, though copies of both epitaphs have been preserved. This second epitaph also gave the date of death as October 23, 1340. However, in the late sixteenth century, two Franciscans, Peter Rudolphus (d. 1586) and Willot (d. 1598), suggested, without documentation, that the date of Lyra's death was actually October 14, 1349. In 1895, J. Viard, National Archivist in Paris, published the treasurer's report of the expenditures of King Philip VI. It records that in July of 1349 payment was made for a keg of wine which the queen gave to Friar Nicholas of Lyra, of the Order of Friars Minor. This later date of death, at least the year, seems more certain and should be accepted.[1] Lyra would then have been about eighty years of age.

II. WORKS AND EDITIONS

Nicholas of Lyra was a prodigious writer. However, there is no agreement about which works attributed to him are authentic and which are spurious, nor their chronological arrangement, nor the exact number of manuscripts and printed editions. The consensus is that the following are authentic: a commentary on Peter Lombard's *Sentences*; two works containing academic disputations on various topics; the *Postilla litteralis*; a résumé of the *Postilla litteralis* for the use of students who (as Lyra says thoughtfully) might not be able to afford the complete *Postilla litteralis* because of its bulk; a response to a Jewish book containing objections to the Christian religion on the grounds of alleged internal evidence in Matthew; the *Postilla moralis*; and a devotion in honor of St. Francis, probably Lyra's last work.

Pertaining to the *Postilla litteralis*, Lyra apparently began to comment on the Book of Genesis in 1322. This date and others are known

---

[1] J. Viard, "La date de la mort de Nicholas de Lyra," *Bibliothèque de l' École des chartes* 56 (1895): 141-43. Many standard reference works still give 1340, e.g., *Oxford Dictionary of the Christian Church*.

because Lyra, unlike most of his contemporaries, dated his commentaries. He completed the *Postilla litteralis* in the early 1330s. What Lyra meant by *litteralis* will be discussed below.

After completing the *Postilla litteralis*, Lyra set to work on the *Postilla moralis*. These were brief, moral, typological, and allegorical notes on passages of Scripture. The work was completed in 1339. Lyra apparently commented on the Song of Songs only once and it is found in both *Postillae*. Quite possibly Lyra's attitude toward the Song was the same as his attitude toward the Epistles which he also explained only once: *sensus litteralis est simpliciter moralis propter quod illas pertranseo* (the literal sense is simply the moral sense, so I will skip them).[2]

The term *postilla* probably comes from *post illa verba* (after these words) and seems to appear for the first time in the commentary of Hugh of St. Cher (ca. 1200-1263). At first the term designated the interpretation of biblical texts in the form of a homily. Later its use was extended to mean the explanation of entire books of the Bible. What Lyra wrote, then, was a "word by word" explanation of the Bible in which he tried to adhere to the literal and later the moral understanding of the text, or perhaps a "running commentary" on the Bible. The German word *Postille* was introduced by Martin Luther.[3]

The *Postilla litteralis* and *Postilla moralis* exist in hundreds of manuscripts, in whole or in part. The printed editions are, according to some scholars, innumerable. The *Postilla litteralis* was the first Bible commentary to be printed, in Rome, in 1471-1472. It passed through at least six editions between 1471 and 1509. Parts were translated into French, German, and Italian before 1500. The last printing was in Paris in 1660. All of this testifies to its popularity.

There exists at present no generally accepted critical edition of any of the works of Nicholas of Lyra. Therefore, "one has to be guided chiefly by convenience," as Beryl Smalley remarked in connection

---

[2] See James George Kiecker, "The Hermeneutical Principles and Exegetial Methods of Nicholas of Lyra, O.F.M. (ca. 1270-1349)" (Ph.D. diss., Marquette University, 1978), 25.

[3] A. Zawart, "The History of Franciscan Preaching and Preachers," *Franciscan Educational Conference, Report of the Ninth Annual Meeting* (Washington, D.C., 1927), 364; *Lexikon für Theologie und Kirche*, 1962 ed., vol. 8, cols. 643-44.

with her own work.[4] The present translation of the Song of Songs is from the *Biblia cum postillis*, 3 vols. (Venice: Franciscus Renner, 1482), vol. 2, extending from fol. 132 recto, col. a. to fol. 138 recto, col. b., in the Archives at Marquette University, Milwaukee. The abbreviated Latin of this text has been transcribed into conventional Latin. Modern punctuation and capitalization have been used, and obvious printing errors have been corrected. In the translation of biblical verses the Douay-Rheims version of the Bible has been used, since it is based quite closely on the Latin Vulgate.[5]

III. THE EXEGETICAL TRADITION PRIOR TO LYRA

The dominant world view from the beginning of Christianity to about the twelfth century was Platonism in one or another of its manifestations. This had a pronounced effect on biblical interpretation. The words, people, and accounts of Scripture were viewed as shadows of higher, spiritual realities. Interpretation of this sort was carried on by the Alexandrine school during the second and third centuries, and became the method of subsequent monastic exegesis.

During the same time period the subordinate world view was derived from Aristotle. Aristotelianism also had an effect on scriptural interpretation, though not yet as pronounced as Platonism. The words of the text, the people and accounts, were not just shadows; they had an intrinsic value worth examining in themselves. The Antiochene approach of the fourth through the sixth centuries was influenced by Aristotelianism.

Late in the tenth century the balance began to tip from the Platonic world view to the Aristotelian. This increased use of Aristotle caused exegesis, formerly done by monks along Platonic lines, to wane; at the same time it caused scholastic exegesis to rise. This shift is most noticeable among the Victorines of the twelfth century.

Scholastic exegesis was carried on by the friars. It was given a methodological underpinning by the Dominican Thomas Aquinas (1225-1274). Aquinas took up the problem of the literal and spiri-

---

[4] Beryl Smalley, *The Study of the Bible in the Middle Ages* (Notre Dame, Ind.: University of Notre Dame Press, 1964), 198, n. 4, continued from page 197.

[5] A reprint of the Straßburg 1492 edition, Nicolaus de Lyra, *Postilla super totam Bibliam* (Frankfurt, 1971), 4 vols., was consulted by the translator.

tual senses in his *Summa theologiae*. God is the principal author of Holy Scripture. Whereas, for human authors, words signify things, for the divine author the things signified by the words signify still other things. When words signify things, the literal sense is intended. When the things signified by the words signify other things, the spiritual sense is intended. The spiritual sense may be divided into the allegorical, the moral, or the anagogical sense, but all are based on the literal sense. The literal and spiritual converge. Futhermore, the literal sense is whatever the author intends. The author may use a metaphor, but intend a literal sense. Therefore the parabolic sense is contained in the literal sense. Only by taking the literal sense seriously, and unlocking it by every means possible, can one hope to grasp the spiritual meaning. Without the literal sense there is no spiritual sense, only vagueness.[6] In his biblical commentaries Aquinas made use of the *Glossa ordinaria* and added a gloss on the Gospels, the *Catena aurea*.

Further attention must be drawn to medieval Jewish exegesis. We have already alluded to Rashi. To the Jewish *midrash*, composed of *halakah* and *haggada*, Rashi added the literal method, with attention to grammar, syntax, philology, chronology, and geography. The school which he founded, about 1070, continued these principles.

IV. LYRA'S ACHIEVEMENT

Lyra's works exhibit both the pre-thirteenth-century, Platonic-motivated, spiritual interpretation of Scripture, and the post-thirteenth-century, Aristotle-motivated, literal interpretation. One is tempted, therefore, to call Lyra a transitional figure. However, his use of the methods developed by his predecessors, his own new insights, and his evident influence on later reformers such as Martin Luther earn Lyra a place among the reformers of biblical exegesis.

Lyra sets forth his hermeneutics in three Prologues, two of which precede his *Postilla litteralis*, and the third which precedes his *Postilla moralis*.[7]

---

[6] Thomas Aquinas, *Summa Theologiae*, ed. and trans. Thomas Gilby, O.P. (New York: Doubleday, Image Books, 1969), vol. 1, pt. 1, quest. 1, art. 10, pp. 59-61.

[7] J.-P. Migne, *Patrologiae, Series Latina*, vol. 113, cols. 25-36, hereafter cited as PL. All translations are mine.

The thrust of the First Prologue is toward the spiritual interpretation of Scripture. The words are not flat, one-dimensional, and are not to be taken only at face value. Rather, they are rich, many-sided, and pregnant with senses. Though Lyra does not mention Thomas Aquinas, he follows Aquinas almost verbatim: God is the principal author of Scripture; he has the power not only to use words to signify things, but to use the things signified by the words to signify still other things. The first signification yields the literal or historical sense. The second yields the spiritual or mystical sense, which is subdivided into the allegorical, the moral or tropological, and the anagogical senses. Lyra then quotes the well-known verse from the schools which summarizes this fourfold sense:

> The literal teaches what happened,
> Allegory is what you believe,
> The moral is what you do,
> Anagogy is where you are heading.[8]

Lyra also refers to the equally familiar fourfold interpretation of the word Jerusalem: literally a particular city, morally the faithful soul, allegorically the Church militant, and anagogically the Church triumphant. In addition, he refers to those passages from Ezekiel and Revelation, so belabored by medieval exegetes, which speak about the "inside" and the "outside" of Scripture.

Lyra's emphasis in the Second Prologue is on the literal sense of Scripture. As he puts it, "Just as a building leaning off its foundation is in danger of collapsing, so a mystical interpretation disconnected from the literal sense is to be considered unsuitable and improper."[9] Though Lyra does not mention Thomas Aquinas, he does mention Rashi, for not only will he make use of Catholic doctors, "but also of the Hebrews, especially of Rabbi Solomon, who among the Hebrew doctors spoke more reasonably in expressing the literal sense."[10]

---

[8] *Littera gesta docet, quid credas allegoria, Moralis quid agas, quo tendas anagogia.* PL 113, col. 28.

[9] *. . . sicut aedificium declinans a fundamento, disponitur ad ruinam: ita expositio mystica discrepans a sensu litterali, reputanda est indecens et inepta . . . .* PL 113, col. 29.

[10] *. . . sed etiam Hebraicorum, maxmine Rabbi Salomonis, qui inter doctores Hebraeos locutus est rationabilem declarationem sensus litteralis inducere.* PL 113, col. 30.

In the course of the Second Prologue which deals with the literal interpretation of Scripture, Lyra refers with approval to seven rules for interpretation which stem from Augustine by way of Isidore of Seville (ca. 560-636). Lyra often gives what seems to be a spiritual interpretation of the scriptural examples which he uses to illustrate these rules. For example, the bridegroom and bride of Isaiah 61:10 (note: an Old Testament reference) are understood as Christ and the Church. The daughters of Jerusalem and Solomon in the Song 1:5 are equated with the Church and God. In Isaiah 14:4, Lyra identifies the King of Babylon with a limb of the devil, and in Isaiah 14:12 he interprets Lucifer as the devil. Since the text itself does not make these identifications, it may seem that Lyra is giving spiritual interpretations. However, if Lyra assumes that the author of the text (ultimately God) *intends* these identifications, then in his own mind Lyra would be giving a literal, not a spiritual, interpretation.

In one instance Lyra seems to make his own original contribution to biblical hermeneutics (with perhaps influence from Aquinas): The same word may have, not a literal and spiritual meaning, but a "double-literal sense" (*duplex sensus litteralis*). In 1 Paralipomenon (1 Chronicles) 17:13, the Lord calls Solomon his son. This is literally so, according to Lyra, because Solomon was God's son by adoption and grace. At the same time, says Lyra, the author of Hebrews 1:5 finds this passage fulfilled in God and his Son. This is also literally so because Christ was God's Son by nature. Lyra grants that Solomon was "less perfectly" a son than Christ, and also concedes that Christ may be a spiritual interpretation of Solomon understood as a "type of Christ." But finally, for Lyra, this passage may be said to have no spiritual sense at all, only a literal. Solomon is literally God's son; Christ is literally God's Son.[11]

---

[11] . . . *eadem littera aliquando habet duplicem sensum litteralem; verbi gratia, primi Paral. XVII dicit Dominus de Salomone: "Ego ero illi in patrem, at ipse erit mihi in filium." Et intelligitur de Salomone ad litteram, inquantum fuit Filius Dei per adoptionem in juventute: propter quod Nathan propheta vocavit eum amabilem Domino, ut habetur secundi Regum XII. Praedicta etiam auctoritas, "Ego ero illi in patrem," etc., inducitur ab Apostolo ad Hebr. primo, tanquam dicta de Christo ad litteram: quod patet ex hoc quia Apostolus inducit eam ad probandum quod Christus fuit major angelis; talis autem probatio non potest fieri per sensum mysticum, ut dicit Augustinus contra Vincentium Donatistam, ut supra allegatum est. Praedicta enim auctoritas impleta fuit ad litteram in Salomone, minus tamen perfecte, quia fuit Dei filius per gratiam solum, in Christo autem perfectius, qui est Dei Filius per naturam. Licet autem utraque*

The thrust of Lyra's Third Prologue (i.e., his Prologue to the *Postilla moralis*) is, like his First Prologue to the *Postilla litteralis*, toward the spiritual interpretation of Scripture. The very designation *moralis* already indicates that. This spiritual thrust is shown in Lyra's treatment of Judges 9:8 ("The trees went to anoint a king over them"), and Jesus' remark in Matthew 5:30 ("If thy right hand scandalize thee, cut it off, and cast it from thee"). In each case Lyra shows there is no literal sense to these passages, only a spiritual. Surely, trees do not literally choose kings, and the Savior does not literally advocate self-mutilation.

Then, in a remarkable about-face, Lyra argues that the above two passages may be understood literally. Taking these passages as parables, Lyra's logic is as follows: When words signify things, the literal sense is present *first*, and if the things signified by the words signify other things, the spiritual sense (in this case the parabolic sense) is present *second*. When words do *not* signify things, i.e., when there is no sense signified by the words, the literal sense is *not* present at all. However, in such cases, if the things signified by the words signify other things, the spiritual (parabolic) sense *is* present, and is in fact the only sense present. Now, whatever sense is present *first* is called the literal sense. Since the spiritual (parabolic) sense is the only sense present, it becomes perforce the *first* sense present. Therefore the spiritual (parabolic) sense becomes the literal sense (*sensus parabolicus est litteralis*). In effect, Lyra is denying the existence of a spiritual sense of Scripture. There is only a literal.[12] But after this sortie into literal interpretation, Lyra returns to dividing the literal and spiritual senses, and continues in this vein until the end of his Third Prologue.

Lyra's treatment of the Song is consistent with the hermeneutical principles he established in his Prologues, particularly in the Third and the Second. The Song is one vast parable and the parabolic sense is the literal sense. Since this is so, one does not look for the spiritual

---

expositio sit litteralis simpliciter secunda tamen, quae est de Christo, spiritualis et mystica est secundum quid inquantum Salomon fuit figura Christi. PL 113, cols. 31 and 32.

[12] . . . *aliqui doctores dicunt sensum parabolicum esse litteralem; hoc est intelligendum large loquendo, quia ubi non est sensus per voces significatus, parabolicus est primus; et ideo large loquendo dicitur litteralis, eo quod litteralis est primus quando non est ibi alius: et ad hoc significandum ipsi dicunt parabolicum contineri sub litterali; et hoc modo loquendo ego sensum parabolicum vocavi in pluribus locis litteralem, scribendo super libros sacrae Scripturae.* PL 113, col. 34.

meaning of the words, but the literal. But this, he says, will be more difficult than in the case of Judges 9. There it was easy to see that the trees and the bramble of the parable referred to the Sichemites and Abimelech literally. But in the case of the Song, it is unclear what the literal meaning of "bride" and "groom" might be.

Lyra rejects various interpretations: He rejects as too fleshly for Scripture the interpretation that the groom and his bride are literally no more than Solomon and Pharaoh's daughter. Likewise he rejects the Jewish interpretation that the groom is literally God and the bride is literally the Jews. He also rejects the Catholic interpretation that the groom is Christ and the bride is the Church. Both Jewish and Catholic interpretations strike Lyra as too narrow. Rather, blending the two, Lyra believes the groom is literally God, and the bride is literally the Church of all ages, God's people in both the Old and New Testaments. Because Lyra believes that the author (ultimately God) *intends* God and his Church by the groom and his bride, he can call his interpretation the literal sense.

But when Lyra interprets "My beloved to me and I to him" as the relationship between the Levites and the Lord (ch. 2:15 and 16); or when he interprets "city" as the desert the Jews crossed, noting that six hundred thousand Jews in the desert would constitute a good-sized city (ch. 3:2); or when "My beloved put his hand through the key hole" is interpreted as God punishing according to his righteousness (ch. 5:4), is he in fact giving a literal interpretation? Rather, it seems that Lyra is giving what long passed for a spiritual interpretation of the Song, but in line with the revolution in exegesis which began about 1100, Lyra is calling his interpretation literal. The method is that of the past, but the terminology is that of the future.

In other ways, too, Lyra's methodology presages the methodology which shortly after his time became associated with the biblical humanists and the reformers. Some examples follow, and the reader of the Song commentary will note others: Lyra's interest in the original Hebrew; his use of Jewish interpretation; his interest in philology and etymology, not always accurately; his development of doctrine on the basis of the text; his interest in geography, botany, social science, medicine, and astronomy; and his use of Scripture to interpret Scripture, a key principle of Reformation exegesis.

Perhaps one might argue that Lyra did a spiritual interpretation of the Song and called it literal. But one can never accuse him of flights of fancy, as is the case of his distant medieval predecessors. Lyra read the text carefully. He tacked the Song firmly to history, i.e., to the Exodus, the journey through the wilderness, and the entry into the Promised Land. The fact that Lyra did not question the historicity of these events may still label him as medieval. But the fact that he was interested in the historicity at all sets him squarely in the history of the reformation of biblical interpretation.

V. LYRA'S INFLUENCE ON LUTHER

An old tradition links Lyra with Luther. On the inside cover of the 1482 edition used for this translation, the phrase *Nisi Lyra Lyrasset, Lutherus non saltasset* (If Lyra had not played his lyre, Luther would not have danced), punning on Lyra's name, appears twice, in different hands. The origin of the phrase, in various forms, is not certain.[13]

Luther refers to Lyra frequently, though ambivalently, throughout his writings. For example, in his 1513 to 1515 Psalms lectures, Luther refers to Lyra several dozen times, and by an overwhelming margin favorably.[14] On the other hand, in his Romans lectures of 1515-1516, Luther's attitude toward Lyra is generally negative. Luther calls his interpretation foolish, false, in error, incorrect, pious but inept, and he dismisses Lyra sarcastically.[15]

By the last decade of his life, Luther's attitude has changed again. In his Genesis lectures Luther refers to Lyra over one hundred times, generally favorably. The passage most often cited by those who wish to show Luther's attitude toward Lyra comes from these lectures: "I

---

[13] Gottfried Edel suggests that the Luther-Lyra verse is probably an adaptation [by someone after Luther's time] from Cornelius à Lapide [1567-1637], "Si Lyra non lyrasset, nemo doctorum in Bibliam saltasset" (Edel, *Das gemeinkatholische mittelalterliche Erbe beim jungen Luther. Beiträge zu einer methodischen Grundlegung* [Marburg: Verlag Dr. R. F. Edel, 1962], 85).

[14] *Luther's Works*, 55 vols. (St. Louis: Concordia Publishing House and Philadelphia: Fortress Press, 1955-1986), vols. 10 and 11. Hereafter this edition is cited as LW.

[15] LW 25:58, 60, 162, 435, 451.

prefer him to almost all other interpreters of Scripture."[16] Luther's ambivalent attitude is summed up in his 1543 lectures on 2 Samuel. Luther calls Lyra an "excellent man," a "good Hebraist," and a "fine Christian," except "whenever he follows his Rabbi Solomon." Then his work becomes "meaningless and unimpressive."[17]

Luther gave his lectures on the Song in 1530 and 1531.[18] Nowhere does he refer to Lyra by name, yet the striking similarities in interpretation suggest that Lyra's commentary lies open before him. Nor does Luther claim to give a literal interpretation. Rather, his goal is "to get at the simplest sense (*simplicissimus . . . sensus*) . . . of this book."[19] Yet the literal sense and the simplest sense turn out to be quite similar.

Like Lyra, Luther admits difficulty in the interpretation of the Song, calling it one of the "obscure books" (*obscuros libros*) in Scripture.[20] Luther rejects a "Solomon-daughter of Pharaoh" interpretation, also a "God - Jews" and a "God - soul" interpretation. For Luther, as for Lyra, God is the bridegroom and his people the bride, all the people of God who possess the Word of God (by implication, thus, similar to Lyra).

Similarities between Luther and Lyra are especially prominent in chapter six. Both find "Turn away thy eyes from me" (v. 4; LW 15:244, v. 5) to be the doublespeak of lovers. Luther takes the sixty queens and eighty concubines (v. 7; LW 15:245, v. 8) to be the wealthier and the more modest cities of Judea; Lyra considers them the synagogues of these cities. Luther and Lyra both interpret "Aminadab" (v. 11; LW 15:247, v. 12) as a noble or ruling people, and connect "soul" with the human will. Both note that "Sulamitis" (v. 12; LW 15:248, v. 13) means perfect.

Similarities between Luther and Lyra are also strong in chapter eight. Both prefer the translation "There your mother bore you" to "There your mother was corrupted" (v. 5; LW 15:257). Luther must have been pleased to see Lyra interpret "My vineyard is before me.

---

[16] LW 2:164. See also *D. Martin Luthers Werke* (Weimar: Hermann Böhlaus Nachfolger, 1883ff.), 42:377: . . . *Scripturae interpretibus eum antepono.* Hereafter this edition is cited as WA.

[17] LW 15:269; WA 54:30.

[18] LW 15:189-264; WA 31,II:586-769.

[19] LW 15:191; WA 31,II:586.

[20] LW 15:194; WA 31,II:588.9.

He let out the same to keepers" (vv. 11 and 12; LW 15:262-63) to mean that God was not turning over the Church to prelates and walking away; both Luther and Lyra still leave God in control. And Luther, like Lyra, finds "gardens" a reference to churches (v. 13; LW 15:263).

But aside from similarities on the level of interpretation, there is similarity on a deeper level, that of total approach to the text. In fact, here we may have the greatest similarity of all; here may lie Lyra's greatest contribution to the reformation of biblical exegesis. We recall Lyra's basic approach: The Song is a parable. The things signified by the words of the Song signify no sense in themselves. It is the things signified by the things signified by the words which signify the sense. And since that sense is the only (and thus the first) sense present, that is the literal sense. Upon this approach Lyra bases his theory that the Song is *literally* about the relation of God to the Church.

Luther's basic approach is strikingly similar. The Song is not merely a love song about the daughter of Pharaoh beloved by Solomon, even if that is what the words indicate. Rather, the words are figurative, to illustrate and adorn a lofty theme.[21] The words of the text are not the literal sense, upon which one may base spiritual senses. Rather, the things signified by the things signified by the words signify the literal sense. When Luther says that the Song is about God and his people, he believes he has found the literal, not the spiritual sense. Of course, Luther does not say that he is giving the *literal* sense of the Song, but its *simplest* sense. But we are suggesting there is very little difference between them. This strong similarity between what Lyra meant by the literal sense (*sensus litteralis*) and what Luther meant by the simplest sense (*sensus simplicissimus*) indicates that Lyra is exerting a definite influence on Luther's biblical hermeneutic. In so doing, Lyra's importance in the history of the reformation of biblical exegesis is established.

As Lyra stretched the limits of literalness, so too Luther stretches the simplest sense. To cite a few examples: When Luther says that "breasts" refer to doctrine (ch. 1:2; LW 15:197); when he interprets "the King has brought me into his chambers" as showing that prayer is heard (ch. 1:4; LW 15:198); the "sun" as tribulation (ch. 1:6; LW

---

[21] Ibid., LW 15:193; WA 31,II:587.

15:203); and "my Beloved is to me a cluster of balsam in the vineyards of Engadi" as "a figurative commendation of the consoling
discovery that God loves, cherishes, protects" (ch. 1:14; LW 15:208),
is this really the simplest sense? Or is it rather what was often considered the spiritual sense? But to suggest this is to miss the point. In
Luther's mind as in Lyra's before him, the logic is clear. What may
seem to be the spiritual is in fact the literal, i.e., the simplest sense.
As Gerhard Ebeling has made clear, the sources of Luther's biblical hermeneutics are manifold.[22] In showing the impact of Lyra on
Luther we perforce indicated the impact that Aquinas and Rashi had
on Luther via Lyra. We have not examined here the impact of, for
example, Faber Stapulensis, and those who may have influenced him.
Then, too, Luther never quite shook off the influence of the medieval fourfold sense of biblical interpretation. Hopefully, we have made
clear only one source, that of Nicholas of Lyra.

---

[22] "Die Anfänge von Luthers Hermeneutik," *Die Zeitschrift für Theologie und
Kirche* 48 (1951): 172-230, trans. Richard B. Steele, "The Beginnings of Luther's
Hermeneutics," *Lutheran Quarterly* 7, no. 2 (summer 1993): 129-158; 7, no. 3
(autumn 1993): 315-338; 7, no. 4 (winter 1993): 451-468.

SELECTED BIBLIOGRAPHY

BOOKS

Augustine. *On Christian Doctrine.* Trans. D. W. Robertson. New York: Bobbs-Merrill, 1958.

Bunte, Wolfgang. *Rabbinische Traditionen bei Nikolaus von Lyra: ein Beitrag zur Schriftauslegung des Spätmittelalters (Judentum und Umwelt,* 58). Frankfurt am Main: Peter Lang, 1994.

Cambridge History of the Bible, vol. 2, "The West from the Fathers to the Reformation." Ed. G. W. H. Lampe. Cambridge: University Press, 1969.

Dahan, Gilbert. *Les intellectuels chrétiens et les juifs au moyen âge.* Paris: Cerf, 1990.

_____. *La polémique chrétienne contre le judaïsme au Moyen Âge.* Paris: Albin Michel, 1991.

De Lubac, Henri. *The Sources of Revelation.* Trans. Luke O'Neill. New York: Herder and Herder, 1968.

Denifle, Heinrich. *Die abendländischen Schriftausleger bis Luther.* Mainz: Kirchheim, 1905.

Glorieux, P. *Répertoire des maîtres en théologie de Paris au XIII͏ᵉ siècle.* 2 vols. Paris: J. Vrin, 1933.

Grant, Robert. *A Short History of the Interpretation of the Bible.* New York: Macmillan, 1948. Macmillan Paperbacks, 1972.

Hailperin, Herman. *Rashi and the Christian Scholars.* Pittsburgh: University of Pittsburgh Press, 1963.

Huizinga, Johan. *The Waning of the Middle Ages.* Trans. F. Hopman. London: Edward Arnold, 1927, 1970.

Kalita, Thomas Marian. "The Influence of Nicholas of Lyra on Martin Luther's Commentary on Genesis." S.T.D. diss., The Catholic University of America, 1985.

Kiecker, James George. "The Hermeneutical Principles and Exegetical Methods of Nicholas of Lyra, O.F.M. (ca. 1270-1349)." Ph.D. diss., Marquette University, 1978.

Krey, Philip Daniel. "Nicholas of Lyra: Apocalypse Commentary as Historiography." Ph.D. diss., University of Chicago, 1990.

Knowles, David. *The Evolution of Medieval Thought*. New York: Random House, Vintage Books, 1962.

Leclercq, Jean, O.S.B. *The Love of Learning and the Desire for God*. Trans. Catharine Misrahi. New York: Fordham Univerity Press, 1974.

Luther, Martin. *D. Martin Luthers Werke*. Weimar: Hermann Böhlaus Nachfolger, 1883ff.

_____. *Luther's Works*. Ed. Jaroslav Pelikan, et al. 55 vols. St. Louis: Concordia Publishing House and Philadelphia: Fortress Press, 1955-1986.

Lyra, Nicholas of. *Biblia cum postillis [Postilla litteralis]*. 3 vols. Venice: Franz Renner, 1482.

_____. *Moralia super totam Bibliam [Postilla moralis]*. Cologne: Johann Koelhoef, 1478.

Migne, J.-P. *Patrologiae, Series Latina*. 221 vols. Paris: Garnier Fratres, 1844-1904.

Reventlow, Henning Graf. *Epochen der Bibelauslegung*. Band II. *Von der Spätantike bis zum Ausgang des Mittelalters*. Munich, 1994.

Smalley, Beryl. *The Study of the Bible in the Middle Ages*. Oxford: Blackwell, 1952; reprinted ed., Notre Dame, Ind.: University of Notre Dame Press, 1964.

Southern, R. W. *The Making of the Middle Ages.* New Haven: Yale University Press, 1968.

Spicq, C. *Esquisse d'une histoire de l'exégèse latine au Moyen Âge.* Paris: J. Vrin, 1944.

Stegmüller, Fridericus. *Repertorium Biblicum Medii Aevi.* 7 vols. Madrid, 1950-61.

Wadding, L., et al. *Annales Minorum.* 32 vols. Florence: Quaracchi, 1931f. Lyra: vols. 2, 5, 6, 7.

_____. *Scriptores Ordinis Minorum.* Rome: F. A. Tanus, 1650.

Dictionaries and Encyclopedias

Biographisch - Bibliographisches Kirchenlexikon, 1993 ed., s.v. "Nikolaus von Lyra," by Klaus Reinhardt.

Dictionnaire de Théologie Catholique, 1926 ed., s.v. "Lyre (Nicolas de)," by F. Vernet.

Encyclopedia Judaica, 1971 ed., s.v. "Nicholas de Lyre," by Raphael Loewe.

Lexicon für Theologie und Kirche, 1962 ed., s.v. "Nikolaus von Lyra" by A. Kleinhans.

New Catholic Dictionary, 1929 ed., s.v. "Nicholas of Lyra," by Cyprian Emanuel.

New Catholic Encyclopedia, 1967 ed., s.v. "Nicholas of Lyra," by J. J. Mahoney.

New Schaff-Herzog Encyclopedia of Religious Knowledge, 1963 ed., s.v. "Lyra, Nicolaus de," by R. Schmid.

Oxford Dictionary of the Christian Church, 2nd ed., s.v. "Nicholas of Lyra."

Religion in Geschichte und Gegenwart, 1960 ed., s.v. "Nikolaus von Lyra," by M. A. Schmidt.

JOURNALS

Anonymous. "Nicolaus von Lyra und seine Stellung in der Geschichte der mittelalterlichen Schrift-Erklärung." *Der Katholik* 2 (Neue Folge, Mainz, 1859): 934-54.

Fischer, M. "Des Nicholaus von Lyra postillae perpetuae in Vetus et Novum testamentum in ihrem eigenthümlichen Unterschied von der gleichzeitigen Schriftauslegung." *Jahrbücher für Protestantische Theologie* 15 (1889): 403-71, 578-619.

Gosselin, Edward A. "A Listing of the Printed Editions of Nicolaus de Lyra." *Traditio* 26 (1970): 399-426.

Labrosse, H. "Nicolas de Lyre." *Études Franciscaines* 16 (1906): 383-404; 17 (1907): 489-505, 593-608; 19 (1908): 41-52, 153-75, 368-79; 35 (1923): 171-87; 400-432.

Langlois, C. V. "Nicholas de Lyre, Frère Mineur." *Histoire littéraire de la France* 36 (1927): 355-400.

Merrill, Eugene H. "Rashi, Nicholas de Lyra, and Christian Exegesis." *Westminster Theological Journal* 38 (1975): 66-79.

Rüthing, H. "Kritische Bemerkungen zu einer mittelalterlichen Biographie des Nikolaus von Lyra." *Archivum Franciscanum Historicum* 60 (1967): 42-54.

Viard, J. "La date de la mort de Nicolas de Lyre." *Bibliothèque de l'École des chartes* 56 (1895): 141-43.

Wood, A. Skevington. "Nicolas of Lyra." *Evangelical Quarterly* 33 (O-D 1961): 196-206.

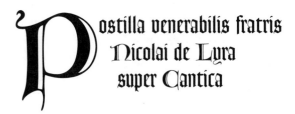

ostilla venerabilis fratris Nicolai de Lyra super Cantica

The *Postilla* of the venerable brother,
Nicholas of Lyra,
on the Song

Cantica

Cap. I.

Osculetur me, etc. Expedito primo Salomonis libro in quo traduntur documenta quae faciunt ad illustrationem mentis, et secundo in quo inducimur ad contemptum affluentiae mobilis, hic consequenter incipit tertius inducens ad amorem supernae felicitatis; sicut dictum fuit plenius in principio primi libri, ubi posui quandam praefationem pro istis tribus libris. Appetitus vero felicitatis supernae procedit ex amore mutuo Dei et rationalis creaturae, qui in hoc libro describitur, ut plenius videbitur prosequendo, tamen ad maiorem dicendorum intelligentiam aliqua sunt hic praemittenda.

Primum est quod translatio nostra in pluribus locis discrepat a littera Hebraica, et similiter signatio capitulorum. Secundum est quod totus iste liber procedit parabolice, nec tamen apparet lucide quibus personis determinatae parabolae secundum sensum litteralem sint applicandae, et hoc cum praedictis difficultatem ingerit in hoc libro. Si enim hoc appareret sicut Iudicum IX, ubi dicitur: Dixerunt autem omnia ligna ad rhamnum, veni et impera super nos, ex littera sequente manifeste patet quod intelligitur de Sichimitis et Abimelech quem unxerunt super se regem, tunc facile esset hunc librum exponere. Sed hoc non apparet nisi in quodam generali, scilicet, quod iste liber loquatur parabolice de amore mutuo sponsi et sponsae, sed quis sit iste sponsus et quae sit haec sponsa, clare non apparet ex littera, propter quod accipiuntur variae a diversis.

Quidam enim dixerunt quod hic accipitur sponsus ad litteram ipse Salomon, et sponsa filia Pharaonis uxor eius praedilecta, sed hoc non videtur verum, quia licet hic amor inter sponsum et sponsam potuerit esse licitus, utpote infra limites matrimonii contentus, sicut dixi plenius super tertium librum Reg., III ca., tamen carnalis fuit, et frequenter habet talis amor aliquid inhonestum et illicitum

THE SONG

The *Postilla* of the venerable brother, Nicholas of Lyra, on the Song.

[Ch. 1:1] *Let him kiss me*, etc. Now that I have finished explaining the First Book of Solomon [Proverbs], which contains lessons to enlighten the mind, and Solomon's Second Book [Ecclesiastes], which teaches us to despise fleeting riches, I turn to his Third Book [the Song], which directs us to seek heavenly bliss. I already explained this quite fully before I began commenting on the First Book, in a preface covering all three books. The desire for heavenly bliss results from the love which exists between God and the rational creature. The Song describes this mutual love, and the comments which accompany the text will make this love even more clear. In order to understand the Song better, some things should be noted.

First, our [Latin] translation frequently disagrees with the Hebrew text and our chapter numbering also differs. Secondly, this whole book is in the form of a parable. However, it is not clear to whom the points of the parable should be applied in order to arrive at the literal sense, and this makes it difficult to interpret this book. It would be easy to interpret if it were, for example, like Judges 9 [14] where it says, "And all the trees said to the bramble, 'Come thou and reign over us.'" Here it is very clear that the text is speaking about the Sichemites and Abimelech, whom the people anointed as their king. But in the case of the Song, the meaning of the text is not clear except in a certain general way. The Song is a parable which speaks about the love between a bridegroom and his bride. But the text does not clearly indicate who this groom and bride might be. Various people have explained the text differently.

Some have said that the groom is literally Solomon, and the bride is the daughter of Pharaoh whom he desired for his wife. But this does not seem to be the correct explanation, because, though such a love between a groom and a bride would be proper, since it is within the bonds of matrimony (as I explained more fully in connection with 3 Kings 3), nevertheless it would be fleshly and often such a love has a certain dishonorable and improper quality about it.

adiunctum, propter quod descriptio talis amoris non videtur ad libros Sacrae Scripturae canonicos pertinere, maxime quia huiusmodi libri Spiritu Sancto dictante sunt scripti.

Salomon autem amorem sui ad uxorem et econverso, et delectamenta ad hoc sequentia cognovit per experientiam et non per Sancti Spiritus revelationem, propter quod hic liber qui semper fuit ab Hebraeis et Latinis inter canonicos libros reputatus, ut patet per Hieronymum in prologo galeato; non videtur de hoc amore conscriptus.

Propter quod Hebraei dicunt quod iste liber loquitur parabolice de amore Dei et plebis Iudaicae, quam sibi desponsavit in legis datione Exo. XX, et sic habuit eam ut sponsam praedilectam. Expositores vero Catholici dicunt communiter, quod iste liber loquitur de amore Christi et Ecclesiae, accipiendo Ecclesiam prout dividitur contra synagogam, quae processit de latere Christi dormientis in cruce, sicut Eva formata fuit de costa dormientis Adae, et sic tam illi quam isti nituntur ad suas intentiones litteram applicare.

Salvo tamen meliori iudicio utriquam videntur in aliquo deficere. Primo in hoc quod sponsam accipiunt nimis stricte Iudaei dicentes sponsam praecise esse plebem Iudaicam cum gente conversa ad ipsam. Catholici vero plebem Christianam, quia in hoc libro ponuntur aliqua quae non videntur convenienter exponi referendo ad statum Veteris Testamenti, et econverso aliqua quae non possunt convenienter exponi de statu Novi. Et ex hoc sequitur defectus alius quo Iudaei aliqua ad statum Novi Testamenti pertinentia inconvenienter exponunt de statu Veteris, et econverso Catholici aliqua ad Vetus Testamentum pertinentia minus convenientur exponunt de statu Novi, loquendo tamen de sensu litterali, cui prout potero insistere intendo.

Et est hic sensus litteralis, non ille qui per voces significatur, sed qui per res significatas primo intelligitur, sicut patet in exemplo supra posito de Abimelech et Sichimitis, propter hoc dicitur parabola a para quod est iuxta, et bole quod est sententia, quia iuxta significationem vocem aliud significatur.

Because of that, the description of such a love does not seem to belong in the canonical books of Sacred Scripture, especially since these
books were dictated by the Holy Spirit. Besides this, Solomon loved
his wife and she loved him, and he learned the delights of this love by
experience, not by the revelation of the Holy Spirit. Therefore, this
book, which has always been included among the canonical books
by the Hebrews and the Latin [translators] —as is clear from Jerome's
defense in his *Prologue* —does not seem to be about such a human
love.

   Hebrew interpreters say that this book is a parable which depicts the love between God and the Jews, a love which was promised
to them at the giving of the Law, in Exodus 20, when God claimed
them as the bride whom he desired. Catholic expositors commonly
say that this book depicts the love between Christ and the Church,
understanding the Church as an entity separate from the synagogue.
They say that the Church originated from the side of Christ "sleeping," [as it were,] on the cross, just as Eve was formed from the rib of
the sleeping Adam, and thus the Catholic interpreters like the Hebrews try to use the text for their own purposes.

   However, carefully considering the matter, both interpretations
seem to be somewhat deficient. First of all, it seems that the Jews
interpret the bride a little too narrowly, saying that she is none other
than the Jewish people and converts to Judaism. The Catholic interpreters also seem to take the bride a little too narrowly, saying she is
only the Christians. But some things in this book cannot be easily
explained with reference to the situation of the Old Testament. On
the other hand, some things cannot be easily explained with reference to the New. Another defect is that the Jews inappropriately apply some things which pertain to the New Testament to the Old,
while conversely Catholic interpreters inappropriately apply some
things from the Old Testament to the New. Each, however, tries to
give the literal sense. It is the literal sense which I intend to present,
to the best of my ability.

   And the literal sense is this, *not* that which is signified by the
words, but that which is signified by the things signified by the words,
just as in the example above about Abimelech and the Sichemites.
This is why the Song is a parable, which comes from *para* meaning
"beside," and *bole* meaning a "thought." For "beside" what is signified, another "word" [or "thought"] is signified.

Igitur in hoc libro sponsus accipi videtur ipse Deus, sponsa vero ipsa Ecclesia complectens statum utriusque Testamenti, quia sicut est una fides modernorum et antiquorum, variata tamen secundum maiorem et minorem explicationem, sic est una Ecclesia variata tamen secundum maiorem et minorem coniunctionem ad Deum, quia magis coniuncta est tempore Novi Testamenti, et hoc modo accipit Ecclesiam beatus Gregorius, Homelia VII, dicens: Quis similitudinem patrisfamilias rectius tenet quam conditor noster qui eos quos condidit sic possidet quasi subditos in domo qui habet vineam, scilicet, universalem Ecclesiam quae a primo Abel iusto usquam ad ultimum electum qui in fine mundi nasciturus est, quot sanctos protulit quasi tot palmites misit. Ecclesia vero sic accepta respicit diversa tempora, et in aliquibus offendit sponsum, et in aliis placavit. Item constituta est ex diversis gentibus, scilicet, ex Iudaeis et Gentibus, ex iustis et peccatoribus, ex praelatis et subditis, et haec et consimilia faciunt difficultatem in hoc libro, quia frequenter fit transitus de uno tempore ad aliud, et de una parte Ecclesiae ad aliam, et de Ecclesia ad Deum et econverso quasi sub eodem contextu litteram, et hoc propter connexionem sponsi et sponsae ad invicem et partium Ecclesiae in unam fidem, sicut plenius dixi in principio Gen. in regulis de intellectu Sacrae Scripturae. Sciendum autem quod licet Ecclesia a principio mundi inceperit, ut praedictum est, tamen specialiter nomen sponsae primo in datione legis in Monte Synai accepit, per quam plebs Israel fuit desponsata Deo per fidem et latriam, aliis gentibus ad idolatriam declinantibus, propter quod Salomon Spiritu Sancto dictante describendo amorem Dei et Ecclesiae sub nominibus sponsi et sponsae, incepit a tempore egressus de Aegyptiaca servitute, quia tunc lex fuit data.

Igitur iste liber dividitur in duas partes, et in prima describitur amor iste pro tempore Veteris Testamenti, et in secunda pro tempore Novi. Secunda incipit infra, ca. VII. Prima dividitur in tres, quia primo describitur amor praedictus prout respicit egressum de terra

So then, in this book, it seems that the groom should be understood as God. The bride, then, is the Church, embracing the circumstances of both Testaments. For just as there is one faith held by modern and ancient people, though there are differences in how clearly things are explained, so there is one Church though there are differences depending on greater or lesser closeness to God, with greater closeness occurring in the time of the New Testament. This is how St. Gregory understood the Church, saying in Homily 7: "What father has a closer relationship to his family than our Creator has to us, owning those whom he created as the inhabitants of his house, which is like a vineyard." This is a reference to the universal Church which extends from Abel, the first just person, all the way to the last elect person who will be born before the end of the world. The Church produces many saints as if they were young grapevines. Thus understood, the Church has a different appearance at different times, depending on whether it has offended the groom or pleased him. Similarly, the Church is composed of different people, that is, Jews and Gentiles, the just and the unjust, those who rule and those who are ruled. This and similar facts cause difficulty in interpreting this book, because frequently there is a transition from one era to another, and from one part of the Church to another, and from the Church to God and God to the Church, interpreting literally. This is due to the connection of the groom and bride alternately to each part of the Church within one common faith, as I explained more fully at [before] the beginning of Genesis, where I set down rules about understanding Sacred Scripture. In addition, one must realize that, though the Church began at the beginning of the world, as I said above, nevertheless it first received the special name "bride" at the giving of the Law on Mt. Sinai, when the people of Israel were betrothed to God by faith and worship, while other nations turned to idolatry. Because of that, when Solomon, as the Holy Spirit dictated to him, describes the love between God and the Church under the names of groom and bride, he begins at the time of the exodus from Egyptian bondage, because it was then that the Law was given.

The Song, therefore, is divided into two parts. The first part describes this mutual love during the time of the Old Testament, and the second part describes it during the New. The second part begins at chapter seven. The first part is divided into three subparts. The first of these describes the love mentioned above, as Solomon looks

Aegypti, secundo progressum per viam deserti, ibi: *Dum esset rex,* tertio ingressum termini, scilicet Iudaeae IIII ca., ibi: *Vadam.* Prima in duas, quia proponitur amorosa sponsae petitio, et gratiosa sponsi responsio, ibi: *Si ignoras.* Prima adhuc in duas, quia proponitur petitio amoris, et exclusio erroris, ibi: *Nigra sum.* Circa primum sciendum quod populus Israel qui sponsae nomine hic intelligitur multum desideravit de Aegypto exire, ut liber a servitute dura posset Deo liberius servire, et ei amore ferventius inhaerere, ut habetur Exo. III, et istud desiderium exprimitur, cum dicitur:

Osculetur me osculo oris sui, id est, utinam Deus ostendat se mihi per signa et effectus amicabilem, sicut sponsum sponsae praedilectae. *Quia meliora sunt ubera tua vino,* in Hebraeo habetur: *Quia meliores sunt amores tui,* nomen enim Hebraicum hic positum equivocum est ad amores et ubera. Hebraei sequuntur unam significationem, translatio nostra aliam, sed in hoc videntur Hebraei melius dicere, quia secundum proprietatem Hebraici sermonis sponsa hic alloquitur sponsum, in commendatione vero sponsi non videtur decenter fieri mentio de uberibus. Potest tamen dici quod per ubera sponsi hic intelligitur plenitudo misericordiae Dei. Est igitur sensus secundum Hebraeos, cum dicitur: *Quia meliores sunt amores tui vino,* id est, sapidiores menti devote quam quodcumquam sapidum corporale gustui corporali. Et secundum translationem nostram: *Meliora sunt ubera tua vino,* id est, tuae misericordiae plenitudo dulcior est humanae menti quam vinum gustui quod inter corporalia est magis sapidum.

Fragrantia, vel *fragrantes* secundum Hebraeos. *Unguentis optimis,* id est, plenitudo tuae misericordiae vel amores tui magis recreant animum devotum quam quodcumquam redolens sensibiliter olfactum. *Oleum effusum nomen tuum,* per oleum hic intelligitur li-

back to the exodus from the land of Egypt. The second of these describes the journey through the desert, beginning with the words, *While the king was [at his repose*, ch. 1:11]. The third of these describes the Jews' arrival at their destination, Judea, in ch. 4 [6], beginning with the words, *I will go [to the mountain of myrrh]*. The first of these three subparts is further divided into two parts. First there is the request of the bride for love, and then the gracious response of the groom, at the words, *If thou know not [thyself*, ch. 1:7]. The first of these two parts is still further divided into two parts. First there is the request for love, and then the removal of error, at the words, *I am black* [ch. 1:4]. Pertaining to the first of these it must be understood that the people of Israel, who are meant here by the name "bride," greatly desired to leave Egypt, so that, free from their hard servitude, they might serve God more freely, and adhere to his love more fervently, as it says in Exodus 3, and this desire is expressed when the text says:

[Ch. 1:1] *Let him kiss me with the kiss of his mouth*, that is, O that God would show his loving self to me by signs and gestures, as a groom does to the bride he desires. *For thy breasts are better than wine*. The Hebrew says, *for thy loves are better [than wine]*. The Hebrew word used here means both "loves" and "breasts." The Hebrew interpreters follow the first meaning, and our [Latin] translation follows the other. But in this case the Hebrew interpreters seem to be on better ground, because, according to the peculiar nature of the Hebrew language, what seems here to be directed to the bride is actually directed to the groom, and, in praising the groom, it does not seem proper to mention his breasts. On the other hand, it might be said that, by the breasts of the groom, the fullness of God's mercy is understood. So, according to the Hebrew interpreters the sense is this: *For thy loves are better than wine*, that is, your love is more delicious to a devout mind than any earthly flavor to the sense of taste. According to our translation the sense is: *[For] thy breasts are better than wine*, that is, the fullness of your mercy is sweeter to the human mind than wine to the sense of taste, wine being among the things that people consider very delicious.

[Ch. 1:2] *The fragrance* or *sweet odors* according to the Hebrews *of the best ointment*, that is, the fullness of your mercy or your love refreshes the devout mind more than anything refreshes the sense of smell. *Thy name is as oil poured out*. "Oil" here is understood as "aro-

quor aromaticus fluens de arboribus aromaticis in Arabia et terra promissionis, et collectus servatur in vasis, et quando effunditur super aliquem ad refrigerium seu medicinam emittit odorem suavem, per quem intelligitur in Scriptura bona fama, secundum illud Apostoli, II Cor. II: Christi bonus odor sumus etc., est igitur sensus cum dicitur: *Oleum effusum* etc., quod per mirabilia quae fecit Deus pro filiis Israel in Aegypto et in Mari Rubro, fama nominis et bonitatis eius diffusa est ad alios populos, propter quam multi ad Iudaismum fuerunt conversi, propter quod subditur: *Ideo adolescentulae dilexerunt te,* id est, aliae gentes ad amorem tuum sunt conversae, multi enim de Aegyptiis hoc modo fuerunt conversi, et cum filiis Israel exierunt de terra Aegypti, ut habetur Exo. XII. Similiter Ietro cum domo sua auditis mirabilibus quae fecerat Deus Israeli Exo. XVIII.

Trahe me post te, educendo me potenter de Aegypto. *Curremus,* te per viam iusticiae sequendo. *In odore unguentorum tuorum,* id est, tracti effectibus bonitatis tuae. Hoc tamen, scilicet, *In odore unguentorum tuorum,* non est de textu, quia non est in Hebraeo, secundum ab aliquo doctore fuit appositum per modum interlinearis glosae, qua postea inserta fuit textui per imperitiam scriptorum. *Introduxit me rex,* caelestis. *In cellaria sua,* revelans mihi per Moysen secreta sua, secundum quod dicitur Exo. III: Cumquam minasset gregem ad interiora deserti etc. Sequitur: Apparuit ei Dominus etc. *Exultabimus et laetabimur in te*, quod fuit impletum quando transito Mari Rubro laetantes dixerunt: Cantemus Domino gloriose etc., Exo. XV. *Memores uberum tuorum,* vel *amorum tuorum* secundum Hebraeos, et exponatur ut supra. *Recti,* id est, iusti. *Diligunt te,* filiali amore.

Nigra sum. Hic consequenter ponitur exclusio erroris. Circa quod sciendum quod Ecclesia militans semper habuit, habet, et habebit usquam ad finem mundi cum iustis aliquos peccatores, et cum fortibus aliquos debiles, propter quod Salvator comparat eam sagenae missae in mare ex omni genere piscium congreganti, Math. XIII, et ideo fragiles Hebraei in Aegypto existentes ex servitute dura per

matic liquid" flowing from sweet-smelling trees in Arabia and in the Promised Land. It is collected and kept in vases, and when it is poured out on anything for refreshment or for healing it gives off a sweet odor. In Scripture a sweet odor stands for a good reputation, as the Apostle says in 2 Corinthians 2 [15]: "For we are the good odor of Christ [unto God]." Therefore, this is the sense of the passage: *[Thy name is as] oil poured out,* for by the wonders which God did for the Israelites in Egypt and in crossing the Red Sea, God's reputation and goodness were spread to other people. Because of this many were converted to Judaism. Therefore the text adds: *Therefore young maidens have loved thee,* that is, other nations were converted to the love of God. Many Egyptians were converted in this way, and they departed from the land of Egypt with the Israelites, as it says in Exodus 12. A similar thing happened with Jethro and his household, when they heard the wonders which God did for Israel, Exodus 18.

[Ch.1:3] *Draw me after thee,* by leading me out of Egypt with a display of power. *We will run,* by following you on the way of righteousness, *to the odor of thy ointments,* that is, we will be drawn by the effects of your goodness. However, this phrase, *to the odor of thy ointments,* does not belong in the [Latin] text because it is not in the Hebrew. Apparently, some doctor wrote this phrase as an interlinear gloss, and later it was inserted into the [Latin] text by scribal error. *The king hath brought me,* that is, the heavenly king, *into his storerooms,* showing me his secrets by means of Moses, as it says in Exodus 3 [1-2]: "And he drove the flock to the inner parts of the desert." After this it says: "And the Lord appeared to him." *We will be glad and rejoice in thee.* This was fulfilled when, after the Israelites had crossed the Red Sea, they rejoiced, saying, "Let us sing to the Lord gloriously," Exodus 15 [1]. *Remembering thy breasts* or *thy loves,* according to the Hebrew interpreters as I explained above. *The righteous,* that is, the just, *love thee,* with childlike love.

[Ch. 1:4] *I am black.* Next comes the removal of error. Pertaining to this, it must be understood that the Church militant always has had, has now, and will have to the end of the world some people who are sinners mingled with the just, and some people who are weak [in faith] along with people who are strong. This is why the Savior compares the Church to a net cast into the sea to catch fish of every kind, Matthew 13. The Hebrews who were weak [in their faith], leading a hard life in Egyptian slavery, and broken down by impa-

impatientiam fracti reputabant totam illam Ecclesiam Deo abominabilem, sicut sponsa deformis viro suo. Cum tamen Deus frequenter permittat electos tribulari ad suam purgationem et meriti augmentationem, propter quod errorem fragilium removet, dicens: *Nigra sum,* id est, turpis in conspectu Dei secundum imperitorum estimationem. *Sed formosa,* secundum veritatem. *Filiae Hierusalem,* id est, O vos imperfecti de plebe Israelitica, propter quod dicuntur filiae in sexu femineo et fragili. *Sicut tabernacula Cedar,* id est, Agarenorum, eo quod Cedar fuit filius Ismaelis, Gen. XXV, qui fuit filius Agar, Gen. XVI. Agareni vero qui nunc dicuntur Sarraceni tunc habitabant in tabernaculis expositis imbribus et nivibus in hyeme, et solis ardoribus in aestate, propter quod denigrata erant exterius, pulchra tamen interius. *Sicut pelles Salomonis,* nomine Salomonis qui pacificus interpretatur, intelligitur ipse Deus secundum Hebraeos, quia disponit omnia suaviter, pelles autem eius dicuntur hic operimentum superius tabernaculi, in quo Deus colebatur, quod erat de pellibus arietum, Exo. XXVI, et erat expositum pluviis et caumatibus, sicut filii Israel duris laboribus in Aegypto.

Nolite me considerare, id est, iudicare. *Quia fusca sim,* id est, obscura et abominabilis Deo. *Quia decoloravit me sol,* mulier enim pulchra de sua natura si solis ardoribus exponatur, a pulchritudine sua exterius immutatur, tamen talis immutatio accidentalis est, et procedit ab exteriori. Est igitur sensus: *Quia decoloravit me sol,* id est, ardor tribulationis Aegyptiacae fecit me nigram et turpem apparere, unde dicitur de hoc ardore, Deut. IIII: Vos autem tulit Dominus et eduxit de fornace ferrea Aegypti, propter quod subditur: *Filii matris meae pugnaverunt contra me,* id est, duris laboribus me afflixerunt Aegyptii qui dicuntur filii eiusdem matris cum Hebraeis, eo quod utriquam de eadem terra fuerunt nati, eo modo loquendi quo nati Parisius dicuntur pueri et filii Parisienses. Omnes enim Hebraei qui cum Iacob fuerunt ingressi Aegyptum, mortui erant quando Aegyptii ceperunt eos affligere, ut habetur Exo. I, et ideo omnes reliqui erant in Aegypto nati. *Posuerunt me custodem vineis,* id est, deputaverunt me servilibus operibus, et forsitan aliqui eorum tanquam servi erant

tience, considered the whole Church to be despised in God's eyes, as a deformed bride is disliked by her husband. However, God frequently permits the elect to be put to the test in order to purge them and to increase their merit. By this means he removes the errors of the weak [in faith]. [The bride says,] *I am black,* that is, I am filthy in the sight of God, in the estimation of ignorant people, *but* in fact *beautiful, O ye daughters of Jerusalem,* that is, O you imperfect ones among the Israelite people, who are called "daughters" to emphasize their weak, feminine-like nature. *As the tents of Cedar,* that is, the tents of the Agareni [Hagar's offspring], because Cedar was the son of Ishmael, Genesis 25, who was the son of Hagar, Genesis 16. The Agareni, who are now called the Saracens, lived at that time in tents exposed to rain and snow in winter and to the sun's heat in summer. This blackened them on the outside, though they were beautiful on the inside. *As the curtains of Solomon.* By "Solomon," which means "peaceful," God himself is meant according to the Hebrew interpreters, because he arranged everything beautifully. The upper covering of the tabernacle in which God dwelt is here called his "curtains," because the tabernacle was covered by curtains, Exodus 26, and was exposed to rain and heat, just as the Israelites were exposed to hard labor in Egypt.

[Ch. 1:5] *Do not consider me,* that is, for the purpose of judging, *that I am brown,* that is, obscure and abominable to God, *because the sun hath altered my color,* for a woman, beautiful by nature, if exposed to the heat of the sun, loses her external beauty. But such a change is accidental and affects only her exterior. Therefore, the sense is: *Because the sun hath altered my color,* this is, the heat of the tribulation in Egypt made me appear black and filthy on the outside only. This heat is mentioned in Deuteronomy 4 [20]: "But the Lord hath taken you and brought you out of the iron furnace of Egypt." In connection with this the text adds, *The sons of my mother have fought against me,* that is, the Egyptians afflicted me with harsh labor. They and the Hebrews are said to be sons of the same mother in the sense that both were born in the same land, the same way that all who are born in Paris are called Parisians. For all the Hebrews who had gone down with Jacob to Egypt had died when the Egyptians began to afflict them, as it says in Exodus 1, so all Hebrews at that time were born in Egypt. *They have made me the keeper in the vineyards,* that is, they appointed me to perform servile tasks; and perhaps some of the He-

deputati nocte et die ad custodiam vinearum. *Vineam meam non custodivi,* id est, operibus meis intendere convenienter non potui propter occupationem in operibus Aegyptiorum.

Indica mihi. Postquam sponsa petivit a sponso dilectionis affectum, hic consequenter petit ab eo directionis effectum. Aliqui enim Hebraei laboribus fracti reputabant Aegyptios felices, et cum eis ad idolatriam inclinabantur, propter quod petit sponsa ab hac deviatione praeservari, dicens: *Indica mihi* etc., et construatur sic litteram: O tu sponse *quem diligit anima mea, indica mihi in meridie,* id est, in hoc tribulationis ardore. *Ubi pascas,* fideles tuos tanquam gregem tuum. *Ubi cubes,* id est, requiescas per fidem formatam, ab infidelitate et idolatria me praeservando, propter quod subditur: *Ne vagari incipiam post greges,* id est, alias gentes infideles. *Sodalium tuorum,* id est, regum et principum ipsarum, qui dicuntur sic sodales Dei, eo quod cum eo participant in nomine, dicuntur enim reges et domini sicut ipse Deus, ut dicit Rabbi Salomon. Sed mihi videtur melius dici quod angeli sancti praelati gentibus infidelibus dicantur hic sodales Dei. Unde Daniel X angelus praelatus Graecis vocatur princeps Graecorum, et praelatus Persis princeps Persarum. Et dicit beatus Dionysius quod fuerunt angeli sancti de quibus certum est quod sunt in societate Dei, et tamen praeerant infidelibus populis.

Si ignoras. Postquam descripta est amorosa sponsae petitio, hic consequenter ponitur sponsi gratiosa responsio, et primo respondet ad petitionem secundam ut continuetur littera ad immediate praecedentem, dicens: *Si ignoras te O pulcherrima inter mulieres,* id est, O tu plebs Hebraea inter alias gentes pulchra propter puritatem fidei et latriae: *Si ignoras te,* id est, times propter infirmos tuos a via recta declinare. *Egredere,* de societate et familiaritate idolatrarum, quia scribitur Proverbia XIII: Amicus stultorum similis efficietur. *Et abi post vestigia gregum,* id est, simplicium credentium quales fuerunt Abel, Seth, Enoch, Noe et consimiles. *Et pasce haedos tuos,* id est, infirmos de populo tuo. *Iuxta tabernacula pastorum,* id est, secundum documenta patriarcharum, qui interrogati de sua conditione

brews, as slaves, were ordered to care for the vineyards night and day. *My vineyard I have not kept,* that is, I was not able to attend easily to my own affairs because I was kept so busy working for the Egyptians.

[Ch. 1:6] *Show me.* After the bride has sought from the groom an expression of love, she next seeks from him some direction. For some Hebrews, broken down by their labors, considered the Eygptians fortunate and turned with them to idolatry. However, the bride sought to be preserved from this sinful deviation, so she says, *Show me,* and adds this statement: O thou groom *whom my soul loveth, show me in the midday,* that is, in the heat of tribulation, *where thou feedest* your faithful people as your flock, *where thou liest,* that is, where you rest by faith which has been formed, by preserving me from infidelity and idolatry. The text then adds, *Lest I begin to wander after the flocks,* that is, after other faithless people, *of thy companions,* that is, after their kings and leaders. They are called companions of God in the sense that they share his name, being called kings and lords, just as God himself, as Rabbi Solomon says. But to me it seems better to say that holy angels, sent to faithless people, are here called the companions of God. So it is in Daniel 10, where the angel sent to the Greeks is called the leader of the Greeks, and the one sent to the Persians is called the leader of the Persians. St. Dionysius says that they were holy angels, so it is certain that they were in the company of God, and still they were in charge of faithless people.

[Ch. 1:7] *If thou know not [thyself].* After the request of the bride for love is described, there follows the gracious response of the groom. First of all he responds to a further request in such a way that the statement ties in with what immediately precedes it, saying, *If thou know not thyself, O fairest among women,* that is, O you Hebrew people, beautiful among other people because of the purity of your faith and worship: *If thou know not thyself,* that is, if you are afraid of departing from the right way because of your weakened condition, *go forth* from association and close ties with idolaters, because it is written in Proverbs 13 [20]: "A friend of fools shall become like to them." *Follow after the steps of the flocks,* that is, follow in the steps of simple believers, such as Abel, Seth, Enoch, Noah, and the like. *And feed thy kids,* that is, those among your people who are weak, *beside the tents of the shepherds,* that is, by following the example of the patriarchs, who, when asked about their occupation, answered, "We

responderunt: *Viri pastores ovium sumus nos et patres nostri* Gen. XLVII.

Equitatui. Hic consequenter respondet ad primam petitionem sponsae quae erat de dilectionis affectione, dicens: *Equitatui meo in curribus Pharaonis assimilavi te amica mea,* id est, ostendi manifeste veram dilectionem ad te quando subverti currus Pharaonis in Mari Rubro te persequentis Exo. XIIII. Et tunc *assimilavi te equitatui meo,* id est, angelis meis quos valde diligo, angeli enim sancti in multis locis Sacrae Scripturae dicuntur eius militia et exercitus, et eodem modo dicuntur hic equitatus Dei. Militum enim turma equitatus communiter nominatur.

Pulchrae sunt genae tuae sicut turturis, id est, pulchritudo fidei tuae est mihi amabilis. In Hebraeo habitur: *Pulchrae sunt genae tuae in ordinibus,* id est, in ornamentis circa faciem tuam ordinate dispositis, et ad hoc consonat litteram sequens cum dicitur: *Collum tuum sicut monilia,* sunt enim monilia colli ornamenta. Hebraei enim de Aegypto exeuntes petierunt ab amicis et vicinis Aegyptiis iocalia argentea et aurea de mandato Dei, Exo. XI, de quibus postea ornaverunt se in solemnitatibus Domini. Ratio vero diversitatis litterae praedictae est, quia nomen Hebraicum ibi positum est equivocum ad turtures et ordines, translatio nostra sequitur primam significationem, Hebraei vero aliam quorum dicto magis consonat littera sequens, ut visum est. Et ad idem pertinet quod subditur:

Murenulas aureas faciemus tibi vermiculatas argento, sunt enim murenulae ornamenta opere plectili facta de filis aureis et argenteis et lapidibus intextis, quibus ornabantur capita mulierum, et orae vestium circa manus et collum.

Dum esset rex. Descripto amore sponsi et sponsae prout respicit exitum de Aegypto, hic consequenter idem describitur prout respicit habitationem in deserto. Et dividitur in duas partes, quia primo ponuntur huius amoris promotiva, secundo eius impeditiva, ut opposita iuxta se posita magis elucescant, secunda pars incipit ibi: *Capite nobis.* Promotiva vero amoris ex parte sponsi sunt eius benefi-

thy servants are shepherds, both we, and our fathers," Genesis 47 [3].

[Ch. 1:8] *To my company of horsemen.* Now the groom replies to the first request of the bride which was for an expression of love, saying, *To my company of horsemen, in Pharaoh's chariots, have I likened thee, O my love,* that is, I showed my true love for you quite clearly when I overturned, in the Red Sea, the chariots of Pharaoh which were following you, Exodus 14. And then he adds, *I have likened thee to my company of horsemen,* that is, to my angels, whom I love very much. For in many places in Sacred Scripture, holy angels are called God's soldiers and army, and in that sense they are here called the company of God's horsemen. For a troop of cavalry soldiers is commonly called a company of horsemen.

[Ch. 1:9] *Thy cheeks are beautiful as the turtledove's,* that is, the beauty of your faith is pleasing to me. The Hebrew text has, *Thy cheeks are beautiful in rows,* that is, in rows of ornamentation circling your face, orderly arranged. This fits in with the statement which follows, *Thy neck as jewels,* since jewels are ornamentation for the neck. Recall that the Hebrews, as they departed from Egypt, by the command of God, sought silver and gold articles from Egyptian friends and neighbors, Exodus 11 [2], with which they later adorned themselves in religious festivals of the Lord. The reason for the different word is the same as explained above [in connection with "breasts" and "loves"]: The Hebrew word used here means both "turtledoves" and "rows." Our [Latin] translation follows the first meaning, but the Hebrew interpreters follow the other. The word "rows" agrees more with the statement which follows, as we saw. It also fits better with the statement which comes after that:

[Ch. 1:10] *We will make thee chains of gold inlaid with silver.* As you know, chain-like decorations are made from gold and silver threads and inlaid stones, woven together. Women adorn their heads with these, and also the borders of their clothing around their hands and necks.

[Ch. 1:11] *While the king was [at his repose].* Solomon, having described the love of the groom and bride in terms of the exodus from Egypt, next describes it in terms of the sojourn in the desert. This is divided into two parts. First come the things which promote this love, followed by the hindrances to it, so that the contrasts, by juxtaposition, stand out more clearly. The second part begins at the words, *Catch us [the little foxes,* ch. 2:15]. The things which cause the

cia in deserto sponsae collata, non tamen recoluntur hic omnia sed
aliqua notabilia, nec ponuntur eodem ordine quo fuerunt collata,
quia frequenter in Sacra Scriptura prius facta posterius narrantur et
econverso. Igitur pars ista dividitur in tres partes, in prima ponitur
beneficium cohabitationis divinae, in secunda columnae nubis et
mannae, ibi: *Sub umbra*, in tertia legis datae, ibi: *Vox dilecti mei*.
Prima adhuc in duas, quia primo ponitur dictum beneficium, secundo
sponsi et sponsae mutuum colloquium, ibi: *Ecce tu pulchra*. Circa
primum sciendum quod maximum beneficium fecit Deus Israeli in
deserto quando voluit habitare in medio populi in tabernaculo in
quo erat propitiatorium tanquam sedes Dei, sicut dictum fuit plenius
Exo. XXV, de quo loquebatur Moysi sicut homo ad amicum suum,
et per Moysen populo, unde dicitur Deut. IIII: Nec est alia natio
tam grandis quae habeat Deos appropinquantes sibi, sicut Deus noster
adest cunctis obsecrationibus nostris. De hac igitur habitatione Dei
dicit sponsa: *Dum esset rex,* caelestis. *In accubitu suo,* id est, in
propitiatorio. *Nardus mea* etc., id est, thymiama boni odoris, quod
offerebatur in altari incensi in conspectu sancti sanctorum ubi erat
propitiatorium.

Fasciculus myrrhae dilectus meus mihi inter ubera mea
commorabitur, id est, intra cor meum per iugena meditationem. Et
dicit *dilectus fasciculus myrrhae,* quia sicut myrrha conservat carnem
a putrefactione, sic Deus mentem a peccati corruptione, et quia non
solum mentem servat sed etiam delectat, ideo subditur:

Botrus etc., et ordinetur sic littera: *Botrus cypri in vineis Engaddi.*
Est autem Engaddi locus ubi crescit balsamum prope Mare Mortu-
um ut apparet in descriptione terrae sanctae, et ibidem crescit arbor
aromatica nomine cyprus, quae facit grana simul iuncta, sicut in uvis
vineae, et inde locus vineae dicitur ut dicunt aliqui. Et ideo cyprus

bride to love the groom are his blessings bestowed on her in the desert. However, not all blessings, but only some noteworthy ones are mentioned here, and they are not arranged in the same order in which they were bestowed, for frequently in Sacred Scripture things done earlier are narrated later, and vice versa. The first part is subdivided into three parts. First comes the blessing of being with God. Second come the pillar of cloud and the manna, beginning at the words *[I sat down] under his shadow* [ch. 2:3]. Third comes the giving of the Law, beginning at the words, *The voice of my beloved* [ch. 2:8]. The first of these three subparts is divided into two additional parts. First there is the word of blessing, followed by the conversation of the groom and bride with each other, beginning at the words, *Behold, thou art fair* [ch. 1:14]. Pertaining to the first of these it should be understood that the greatest blessing God bestowed on Israel in the desert was deigning to live in the midst of his people in the tabernacle where the place of propitiation was located, as it were the very seat of God, as was explained more fully in connection with Exodus 25. From this place God spoke to Moses as a person to a friend, and through Moses, God spoke to the people. This is why it says in Deuteronomy 4 [7]: "Neither is there any other nation so great, that hath gods so nigh them, as our God is present to all of our petitions." Pertaining to the place where God dwelt, the bride says, *While the king,* of heaven, *was at his repose,* that is, in the place of propitiation, *my spikenard [sent forth the odor thereof],* that is, thyme which has a pleasant odor. This was offered at the altar of incense in front of the holy of holies, where the place of propitiation was located.

[Ch. 1:12] *A bundle of myrrh is my beloved to me, he shall abide between my breasts,* that is, within my heart, by my continual meditation. The text says, *A bundle of myrrh is my beloved,* because, just as myrrh keeps meat from spoiling, so God keeps the mind from being corrupted by sin. Furthermore, because God not only keeps the mind, but also pleases it, this follows:

[Ch. 1:13] *A cluster [of cypress my love is to me].* The scope of this statement is then narrowed: *A cluster of cypress in the vineyards of Engaddi.* Now, Engaddi is a place near the Dead Sea where balsam grows, as can be learned from the description of the Holy Land. There an aromatic tree also grows called the cypress, which produces seeds packed tightly together just like a cluster of grapes on a vine. Because of that, some call Engaddi the place of the vine. Cypress here is not

non est hic nomen insulae quae est in Mari Mediterraneo, quia ibi non sunt dictae vineae. *Dilectus meus mihi,* id est, magis delectat me spiritualiter quam quodcumquam sapidum et suave delectat corporaliter.

Ecce tu pulchra es. Post cohabitationem sponsi et sponsae ponitur hic mutuum colloquium gratiosum sponsi et sponsae, quod solet esse in corporalibus ex cohabitatione, et secundum hoc dicit sponsus: *Ecce tu pulchra es amica mea* etc., et duplicatur littera pulchra ad denotandum pulchritudinem mentis et exterioris conversationis. *Oculi tui columbarum,* per simplicem contuitum, qui multum decorat sponsam corporalem, et per hoc in sponsa spirituali simplicitas intentionis intelligitur eam decorans, secundum quod dicit Salvator, Math. VI: Si oculus tuus fuerit simplex, totum corpus tuum lucidum erit, et respondet sponsa:

Ecce tu pulcher es dilecte mi et decorus, cuius pulchritudinis non est finis. *Lectulus noster,* id est, tabernaculum in quo sponsa per Moysen et Aaron et alios sacerdotes in quietae contemplationis quasi in lecto quiescebat. *Floridus,* quia operimentum interius tabernaculi erat de cortinis variis coloribus et pulchra varietate contextis ad modum diversorum florum, Exo. XXVI, et quia templum Salomonis postea fuit aedificatum ad similitudinem huius tabernaculi, ideo occasione huius dicitur hic de ipso:

Tigna domorum nostrarum cedrina etc., de talibus enim lignis fuit illud templum aedificatum, ut patet III Reg., et subdit sponsa tanquam de beneficiis sponsi grata:

Ego flos campi, id est, modo habito pura et munda extra vilitatem Aegypti. *Et lilium convallium,* quasi diceret, quando eram in Aegypto, eram quasi lilium in monte, cuius color obfuscatur solis ardore, sicut dixit supra. *Decoloravit me sol.* Sed modo sum sicut lilium in valle, quod habet colorem recentem ex vallis humore, et quia Deo placet sponsae gratitudo, ideo subdit eam commendando:

Sicut lilium inter spinas, id est, sicut lilium redolens et suave comparatur ad spinas asperas et pungentes: *Sic amica mea,* id est, plebs Hebraica. *Inter filias,* id est, gentes alias quae sunt idolatriae deditae, et innocentes tractant asperae, sicut patet de Aegyptiis qui tractaverant Hebraeos valde dure, et subditur responsio sponsae:

the name of the island [Cyprus], which is in the Mediterranean Sea. *My beloved is to me,* that is, he pleases me more in a spiritual way than anything wise or pleasant pleases me bodily.

[Ch. 1:14] *Beloved, thou art fair.* After the sexual relations of the groom and bride, we now have their mutual and gracious conversation, the kind which usually follows that activity. The groom says, *Behold, thou art fair, O my love,* and the word "fair" is repeated to denote the beauty of mind internally to go with the pleasantness of conversation externally. *Thy eyes are those of doves* by the way they gaze undistractedly upon the groom, which adds much to the physical beauty of the bride. This means the bride's singleminded, spiritual attention, which adds to her adornment, as the Savior says in Matthew 6 [12]: "If thy eye be single, thy whole body shall be lightsome." The bride responds:

[Ch. 1:15] *Behold, thou art fair, my beloved, and comely;* of his fairness there is no end. *Our bed,* that is, the tabernacle where the bride through Moses and Aaron and other priests rested in quiet contemplation, *was bedecked with flowers;* for the inner covering of the tabernacle consisted of variously colored curtains, embroidered with a variety of beautiful flowers, Exodus 26. Because Solomon's temple later on was modeled on the tabernacle, the following is said about it:

[Ch. 1:16] *The beams of our houses are of cedar,* since the temple was built from this wood, as 3 Kings shows. The bride adds, as it were, thanks for the blessings of the groom:

[Ch. 2:1] *I am the flower of the field,* that is, I now live purified and cleansed, away from the vileness of Egypt, *and the lily of the valleys,* as if she would say: When I was in Egypt, I was like a lily on the mountain, whose color has been faded by the harshness of the sun. As the bride said earlier, *The sun hath altered my color* [ch. 1:5]. But now I am like a lily in the valley, which has received color from the valley's moisture. Because the thanks which the bride offers pleases God, he praises her, saying:

[Ch. 2:2] *As the lily among thorns,* that is, as a lily, sweet-smelling and pleasant, stands out from sharp and foul-smelling thorns, *so is my love,* that is, the Hebrews, *among the daughters,* that is, the other nations, which are given to idolatry and bring the innocent to ruin, as can be seen from the extremely harsh way that the Egyptians treated the Hebrews. The bride's reply follows:

Sicut malus, quae est arbor fructifera. *Inter ligna silvarum,* quae communiter sunt infructifera. *Sic dilectus meus,* a quo procedunt cuncta bona. *Inter filios,* id est, aliarum gentium deos a quibus nulla bonitas procedit, secundum sunt inutiles omnino.

Cap. II.

Sub umbra illius. Hic consequenter ponitur duplex notabile beneficium in deserto Israeli exhibitum. Primum est beneficium columnae ignis et nubis quae illuminabat noctem, et de die temperabat solis ardorem, Exo. XIII, et quantum ad hoc dicit sponsa: *Sub umbra illius quem desiderabam sedi,* id est, mansi vel habitavi, sicut dicitur Deut. I, Sedistis ergo in cadesbarne multo tempore, id est, mansistis. Secundum beneficium fuit mannae caelitus datae in cibum, Exo. XVI. De quo cibo dicitur Sapie. XVI: Panem paratum de caelo praestitisti eis sine labore omne delectamentum in se habentem et omnis saporis suavitatem, et hoc est quod subditur: *Fructus eius dulcis gutturi meo.* Tertium beneficium fuit ritus sacrificiorum per quae placabatur offensa divina, et conferebatur gratia, non ex sacrificiis secundum se: sed inquantum fiebant ex offerentium fide et devotione et quantum ad hoc dicit sponsa:

Introduxit me rex in cellam vinariam, id est, ad altare holocaustorum, ut dicit Rabbi Salomon quod dicitur cella vinaria, eo quod in libaminibus sacrificiorum ibi effundebatur vinum, et tunc Levitae cantores incipiebant canere divinas laudes quae ordinantur ad dilectionem Dei et proximi, ideo sequitur: *Ordinavit in me caritatem.* Licet autem per caritatem Deus habeatur in via, hoc tamen non est in re per quem modum habetur in patria, sed in spe. Licet autem spes inquantum est de bono causet delectationem, tamen absentia realis huius boni inducit afflictionem, secundum illud Prov. XIII: Spes quae differtur affligit animam, et haec afflictio vocatur hic languor sponsae. Mulier autem languida corporaliter delectatur florum et pomorum odoribus et sponsi amplexibus, per quae hic designantur metaphorice divinae consolationes quae dantur sperantibus in se, cum dicitur:

[Ch. 2:3a] *As the apple tree,* which is a fruit-bearing tree, *among the trees of the woods,* which usually are not fruit bearing, *so is my beloved,* from whom come all good things, *among the sons,* that is, the gods of the nations, from whom comes no goodness at all, and so are in all respects useless.

[Ch. 2:3b] *Under his shadow.* Next comes a double, notable blessing bestowed on Israel in the desert, first the blessing of the pillars of fire and cloud, which illuminated the night, and tempered the sun's heat by day, Exodus 13. Pertaining to this blessing the bride says, *I sat down under his shadow, whom I desired,* that is, I sat there or I lived there, as it says in Deuteronomy 1 [6]: "You have sat long enough on this mountain," that is, you have lived there. A second blessing was the heavenly manna given for food, Exodus 16, about which Wisdom 16 [20] says: "Thou didst feed thy people with the food of angels, and gavest them bread from heaven prepared without labor, having in it all that is delicious, and the sweetness of every taste." And this follows: *And his fruit was sweet to my palate.* A third blessing was the sacrificial rites by which God, who had been offended, was appeased and grace was given, not by the sacrifices themselves, but only insofar as the ones who made the offerings did so out of faith and devotion. Pertaining to this the bride says:

[Ch. 2:4] *The king brought me into the cellar of wine,* that is, to the altar of burnt offerings. As Rabbi Solomon says, this altar is called "the cellar of wine" because wine was poured out there in sacrificial libations, and then the Levitical cantors began to sing divine praises which were intended to show love for God and the neighbor. Therefore it follows: *He set in order charity in me.* The Israelites possessed God by love for him on their journey, but this is not how they possessed him once they got to the homeland; rather, they then possessed him in hope. Hope, insofar as it arises from goodness, produces delight. However, the absence of this true goodness leads to affliction, according to Proverbs 13 [12]: "Hope that is deferred afflicteth the soul." And this affliction is here called the languor of the bride. The wife, languid in body because of her love, is pleased with the odors of the flowers and the apples, and with the embraces of the groom. Metaphorically, this means the consolations which God gives to those who are filled with hope. Then the text says:

Fulcite me floribus, stipate me malis etc., et patet ex dictis littera. Et quia continuatio talium consolationum est appetenda et subtractio abhorrenda, ideo subditur:

Adiuro vos filiae Hierusalem, id est, infirmi de populo Israel, ut dictum est supra, ca. I. *Per capreas cervosque camporum,* id est, per patriarchas qui sic nominantur in Scriptura, Gen. XLIX: Neptalim cervus emissus etc. *Ne suscitetis neque evigilare faciatis dilectam,* id est, ut non declinetis ad aliquod horribile peccatum, propter quod divina consolatio subtrahatur et totus populus perturbetur, sicut contigit in fabricatione vituli et euis adoratione, Exo. XXXII. *Donec ipsa velit,* per istud donec non intelligitur quod sponsa debeat hoc velle futuro tempore, sicut Math. I, de Ioseph et Maria dicitur: Et non cognoscebat eam donec peperit, quia non cognovit eam postea.

Vox dilecti mei. Hic ponitur beneficium datae legis, quod fuit valde gratiosum vel notabile, secudum quod dicitur Deut. IIII: Non est enim alia gens sic inclyta ut habeat cerimonias iustaque iudicia et universam legem etc. De hoc beneficio dicit hic sponsa: *Vox dilecti mei,* pronunciantis praecepta decalogi, Exo. XX. Locutusque est Dominus cunctos sermones hos: Ego sum etc. *Ecce iste venit saliens in montibus,* id est, descendens in Montem Synai in quo protulit praecepta decalogi, qui dicitur montes et colles in plurali propter diversas sui partes, vel ponendo plurale pro singulari, sicut frequenter fit in Scriptura, unde Exo. XXXII: Isti sunt de tui Israel, quid eduxerunt te de terra Aegypti, et tamen erat ibi unum idolum tantum.

Similis est dilectus meus capreae hinnuloque cervorum, per hoc designatur velocitas divini descensus ad dandum legem. *En ipse stat post parietem nostrum.* Per parietem intelligitur nubes densa quae inter Deum erat et populum, et quia ex illa nube procedebant coruscationes ex quibus videbatur nubes aperiti, ideo subditur: *Respiciens per fenestras prospiciens per cancellos,* scilicet, illius nubis aperturas, quia concutiebatur populus timore, ac si Deus praesentialiter videretur, unde Exo. XX dicitur: Cunctus autem

[Ch. 2:5-6] *Stay me up with flowers, compass me about with apples,* etc. The meaning of these words is clear. Because the continuation of such divine consolation is to be sought, and its removal is to be avoided, the text adds:

[Ch. 2:7] *I adjure you, O ye daughters of Jerusalem,* that is, you among the Israelites who are weak, as I explained above in chapter one, *by the roes and the harts of the fields,* that is, by the patriarchs who are called this in Scripture, Genesis 49 [21]: "Naphtali, a hart let loose," *that you stir not up, nor make the beloved to awake,* that is, that you not be inclined to commit some terrible sin, because of which divine consolation might be withdrawn, and the whole nation be troubled, which in fact happened when the calf was set up and worshiped, Exodus 32. *Till she please:* "Till" should not be understood to .mean that the bride might wish this at a future time, but rather "till" in the sense that it is used in Matthew 1 [25] about Joseph and Mary: "And he knew her not till she brought forth." For Joseph did not know her afterwards either.

[Ch. 2:8] *The voice of my beloved.* This refers to the blessing of the giving of the Law, which was an especially gracious and noteworthy act, as it says in Deuteronomy 4 [8]: "For what other nation is there so renowned that hath ceremonies, and just judgments and all the law, etc.?" Pertaining to this blessing the bride says: *The voice of my beloved,* pronouncing the precepts of the decalogue, Exodus 20 [1-2]: "And the Lord spoke all these words: I am, etc." *Behold, he cometh leaping upon the mountains,* that is, descending upon Mt. Sinai, where he gave the precepts of the decalogue. Mt. Sinai is called "mountains" and "hills" in the plural because of the various parts of it; or perhaps here is a case of the use of the plural for the singular, as Scripture does frequently. For example, Exodus 32 [4] states: "These are thy gods, O Israel, that have brought thee out of the land of Egypt." Yet there was only one idol.

[Ch. 2:9] *My beloved is like a roe, or a young hart.* This refers to the swiftness of God's descent when he gave the Law. *Behold, he standeth behind our wall.* "Wall" refers to the dense cloud which stood between God and the people. And because the lightening flashing forth from that cloud seemed to rend the cloud apart, this is added: *looking through the windows, looking through the lattices,* that is, the openings in the cloud. This event struck the people with fear; it was as if they were seeing God in person. This is found in Exodus 20

populus videbat voces et lampades, id est, coruscationes. Sequitur ibidem: *Et territi ac pavore concussi procul stantes dixerunt Moysi: Loquere tu nobis, et audiemus, et non loquatur nobis Dominus ne forte moriamur.*

En dilectus meus loquitur mihi. Surge propera, id est, animum erige ad verba mea. *Amica mea,* per caritatem. *Columba mea,* per intentionis simplicitatem. *Formosa mea,* per exteriorem honestatem. *Et veni,* ad serviendum mihi soli, unde primum praeceptum decalogi est: Non habebis deos alienos coram me etc., et subditur ratio:

Iam enim hyems transiit imber abiit et recessit, id est, tempus horridum Aegpytiacae servitutis in quo a servitute mea impediebaris.

Flores apparuerunt in terra nostra etc., id est, tempus amoenum libertatis venit, in quo libere potes mihi servire. Hoc autem tempus libertatis intelligitur hic per tempus vernale, in quo incipiunt flores apparere, turtures cantare, et aves cetere, vineae florere in terra illa quae est valde calida, arbores putari, et primae ficus maturari, et secundum veritatem historiae populus Israel exivit de Aegypto in vere. Exivit enim XV die mensis primi qui incipit a prima lunatione propinquiori equi noctio vernali, ut dixi plenius Gen. VII et Exo. XII, et quinquagesima die ab exitu fuit data lex in Monte Synai.

Surge propera etc., exponatur ut supra, quia repetitio est eiusdem ad maiorem excitationem.

Columba mea. Hic incipit versus in Hebraeo. Columba enim nidificat *in foraminibus* parietum et petrarum, per quae designatur hic locus castrorum, ubi populus Israel habitabat. Est igitur sensus: *Columba mea,* id est, plebs Hebraica, ut praedictum est. *In foraminibus petrae in caverna maceriae,* id est, in habitaculis tuis. *Ostende mihi faciem tuam,* hilariter recipiendo legem meam. *Sonet vox tua in auribus meis,* profitendo conservationem meae legis, secundum quod scribitur Exo. XXIIII: Venit ergo Moyses et narravit plebi omnia verba Domini atque iudicia, responditque populus cunctus una voce: Omnia verba Domini quae locutus est faciemus, et quia hoc fuit Deo placitum, ideo subditur: *Vox enim tua dulcis* etc.

[18]: "And all the people saw the voices and the flames," that is, the lightening flashes. That passage continues: "And being terrified and struck with fear, they stood afar off, [19] saying to Moses: 'Speak thou to us, and we will hear: let not the Lord speak to us, lest we die.'"

[Ch. 2:10] *Behold, my beloved speaketh to me: Arise, make haste.* This means, lift up your spirit at my words, *my love,* that is, by means of love, *my dove,* by undivided attention, *my beautiful one,* by outward decency, *and come,* to serve me alone. As the first precept of the decalogue states: "Thou shalt not have strange gods before me" etc. [Exod. 20:3]. The reason why this should be done follows:

[Ch. 2:11] *For the winter is now past, the rain is over and gone,* that is, the terrible time of Egyptian slavery, during which you were prevented from serving me.

[Ch. 2:12] *The flowers have appeared in our land* etc., that is, a delightful time of freedom has come, during which you are able to serve me freely. This time of freedom is indicated here by the springtime, when the flowers begin to appear, the turtledoves to sing, the birds to fly, the vines to blossom, the trees to bud, and the first figs to mature, in that land which ordinarily is very hot. As a matter of historical fact, the Israelites left Egypt in the spring. They made their exodus on the fifteenth day of the first month which begins at the appearance of the moon closest to the vernal equinox, as I explained more fully in my comments on Genesis 7 and Exodus 12. Fifty days after the exodus the Law was given on Mt. Sinai.

[Ch. 2:13] *Arise and come* etc. is understood as above. The repetition of the same words is to enhance the excitement.

[Ch. 2:14] *My dove.* In the Hebrew the verse begins with this word. For a dove dwells in the cracks of walls and rocks, which refer to the camps where the Israelites lived. So the sense is this: *My dove,* that is, my Hebrew people, as I just explained, *in the clefts of the rocks, in the hollow place of the wall,* that is, in your small dwelling places, *show me thy face,* by receiving my Law with joy. *Let thy voice sound in my ears,* by promising to keep my Law, as it says in Exodus 24 [3]: "So Moses came and told the people all the words of the Lord, and all the judgments: and all the people answered with one voice: 'We will do all the words of the Lord, which he hath spoken.'" Since this action was pleasing to God, this follows: *for thy voice is sweet* etc.

Capite nobis. Post amoris sponsi et sponsae promotiva hic interseruntur impeditiva, et licet plura fuerint in deserto ubi populus pluries offendit Deum, tamen hic ponuntur duo magis notabilia, secundum ibi: *In lectulo meo.* Primum autem impedimentum est de adoratione vituli, quod fuit maximum, ad quod inductus fuit populus per aliquos ad idolatriam magis pronos, et fraudulenter sub specie boni dicentes Aaron Exo. XXXII: Fac nobis deos qui praecedant nos: Moysi enim viro huic qui nos eduxit de terra Aegypti, nescimus quid acciderit, quasi dicant, non possumus procedere sine ductore, et isti postea fuerunt interfecti per Levitas, ut ibidem habetur, et hoc est quod hic dicitur: *Capite nobis,* id est, interficite. *Vulpes parvulas quaedemoliuntur vineas,* id est, personas dolose inducentes populum ad idolatriam. *Nam vinea nostra,* id est, plebs Israelitica, Isaias V: Vinea Domini exercituum domus Israel est. *Floruit,* floruerat enim haec vinea in receptione legis devota, et sicut tempore floritionis vineae vulpes ibi transeuntes et flores excutientes faciunt magnum damnum, sic praedicti idolatrae in vinea Israel fecerunt magnum damnum spirituale. Verumtamen quia Levitae iunxerunt se cum Domino et Moyse, Exo. XXXII: Si quis est Domini iungatur mihi: congregatique sunt ad eum omnes filii Levi, qui erant pars notabilis populi, ideo in persona eorum dicit sponsa:

Dilectus meus mihi et ego illi, et non vitulo conflatili. *Qui pascitur inter lilia,* id est, delectatur in personis mundis ab idolatria.

Donec aspiret dies, scilicet, expiationis, in quo ad preces Moysi Dominus fuit placatus populo de peccato vituli, propter quod subditur: *Et inclinentur umbrae,* in Hebraeo habetur: *Fugiant umbrae,* id est, dicti peccati maculae, et propter Dei placationem subdit sponsa: *Revertere dilecte mi,* diligendo me sicut prius. *Similis esto* etc., id est, fac istud celeriter. *Super montes Bethel,* id est, super Montem Synai ubi Dominus loquebatur Moysi, qui dicitur montes in plurali

[Ch. 2:15] *Catch us.* After mentioning the things which arouse love between the groom and bride, the things which hinder their love are now included. Of course, there were many such hindrances in the desert, where the people so often offended God. But here only two of the more noteworthy are mentioned. The second one begins at the words, *In my bed* [ch. 3:1]. The first hindrance [to their love], which was the worst, was the worship of the calf. The people were led by men who were very much inclined towards idolatry. These men said to Aaron, cunningly, under the guise of good intentions, in Exodus 32 [1]: "Make us gods, that may go before us: for as to this Moses, the man that brought us out of the land of Egypt, we know not what has befallen him," as if they were saying, "We are not able to go on without a leader." Afterwards, these same men were killed by the Levites, as that same passage informs us, so what is meant here is this: *Catch us,* that is, kill, *the little foxes that destroy the vines,* that is, those persons who cunningly led the people into idolatry. *For our vineyard,* that is, the Israelites, as in Isaiah 5 [7]: "For the vineyard of the Lord of hosts is the house of Israel." *Hath flourished*; it flourished because this vineyard accepted devoutly the Law. Just as wolves, running through a vineyard in blossom, cause great damage by knocking off the blossoms, so the above-mentioned idolaters caused great spiritual damage in the vineyard of Israel. However, since the Levites stood firmly with the Lord and with Moses (as it says in Exod. 32 [16]: "If any man be on the Lord's side, let him join with me. And all the sons of Levi, who were a notable part of the people, gathered themselves together unto him"), therefore the bride in the person of them says:

[Ch. 2:16] *My beloved to me, and I to him,* [that is, I am committed to him] not to a calf that can be burned, *who feedeth among the lilies,* that is, he who deals favorably with people who have not committed idolatry.

[Ch. 2:17] *Till the day break,* that is, the Day of Atonement, when, by Moses' intercessions, the Lord was reconciled to the people in regard to their sin of worshiping the calf. Therefore this phrase follows: *and the shadows retire.* The Hebrew text says, *and the shadows flee,* that is, the stains of sin. And because God was appeased, the bride adds: *Return, my beloved,* by desiring me as you did at first. *Be like [to a roe, or to a young hart],* that is, do this swiftly, *upon the mountains of Bethel,* that is, upon Mt. Sinai where the Lord spoke to Moses. It is

rationibus supradictis, et dicitur mons Bethel, id est, domus Dei, quia habitavit ibi cum Moyse. Tamen in Hebraeo habetur: *Super montes Bathar,* id est, partitionis vel separatonis, scilicet, Dei a populo, ut dicit hic Rabbi Salomon, quia tunc temporis dixit Dominus Moysi: Vade et descende de loco isto peccavit populus tuus etc., et sequitur: Non enim ascendam tecum, quia populus durae cervicis est, tamen finaliter ad preces Moysi concessit se esse ductorem populi.

Cap. III.

In lectulo meo. Hic ponitur secundum impedimentum quod contigit per exploratores qui terruerunt populum in tantum quod dimisso Moyse et archa Dominus voluerunt reverti in Aegyptum, dicentes Numeri XIIII: Constituamus nobis ducem et revertamur in Aegyptum, propter quod Dominus iratus dedit sententiam irretractibilem, quod omnes egressi de Aegypto a XX annis et supra, morerentur in deserto praeter Caleph et Iosue, et hoc impedimentum lamentatur sponsa, dicens: *In lectulo meo,* id est, in Moysi tabernaculo, ut dictum est supra, I ca. *Per noctem,* id est, tempore tribulationis excitate per exploratores. *Quaesivi quem diligit,* Moyses enim et Aaron in tabernaculo oraverunt Dominum pro populo ut dicta sententia temperaretur, sed quia non fuerunt exauditi, ideo subditur: *Quaesivi illum et non inveni* etc.

Surgam et circuibo civitatem, id est, desertum annis XL, quod licet non possit dici civitas secundum se acceptum tamen dicitur civitas propter multitudinem populi ibi circumeuntis, in qua erant sexcenta milia absque mulieribus et parvulis. *Per vicos et plateas* etc., quia in omni loco ad quem populus declinabat implorabat Dei misericordiam. Et consequenter revertitur ad factum Moysi et Aaron, dicens:

Invenerunt me vigiles, id est, Moyses et Aaron, ut dicitur hic Rabbi Salomon eo quod vigilabant super custodiam populi et annunciaverunt populo sententiam Domini. Sed quia die sequenti

called "mountains" in the plural for the reasons I suggested above. The mountain is called "Bethel," that is, the house of God, because God dwelt there with Moses. However, the Hebrew says, *upon the mountains of Bathar,* that is, the mountains of partition or separation, referring to the separation of God from the people, as Rabbi Solomon interprets it; because of the time the Lord said to Moses [Exod. 32:7]: "Go, get thee down, thy people hath sinned." The reason is also given [Exod. 32:9]: "For I will not go up with you, because this people is stiffnecked." Finally, however, God gave in to the prayers of Moses that God continue to be the Israelite leader.

[Ch. 3:1] *In my bed.* We come to the second thing that hindered [the Israelites in their love for God, that is, collectively,] the tests which disheartened the people so much that, no longer having confidence in Moses and the ark of the Lord, they wanted to return to Egypt. As they said in Numbers 14 [4]: "Let us appoint a captain, and let us return into Egypt." Because of this, the Lord, filled with anger, gave an irretractable sentence: All who left Egypt twenty years of age and older would die in the desert, except Caleb and Joshua. Because this incident stood in the way of mutual love between the groom and bride, the bride laments, saying, *In my bed,* that is, in Moses' tabernacle, as I explained above in chapter one, *by night,* that is, during the time of tribulation caused by these tests, *I sought him whom [my soul] loveth.* Recall that Moses and Aaron prayed in the tabernacle to the Lord on behalf of the people, that God would temper this sentence. But because they were not heard, the text adds: *I sought him, and found him not.*

[Ch. 3:2] *I will rise, and will go about the city,* that is, I will wander in the desert for forty years, because, though a desert cannot be called a city in the usual sense, nevertheless it is here called a city because of the number of people wandering about in it. In this "city" there were 600,000 men not counting women and children. *In the streets and the broad ways [I will seek him whom my soul loveth: I sought him, and I found him not],* because everywhere the people turned they implored the mercy of God. Next the text returns to what Moses and Aaron did, saying:

[Ch. 3:3] *The watchmen [who keep the city] found me,* that is, Moses and Aaron, as Rabbi Solomon interprets it, in the sense that they watched over the well-being of the people and they announced to the people the Lord's sentence. But because on the following day

populus penitens de dicta rebellione, dixit: Parati sumus ascendere ad locum de quo locutus est Dominus: Quia peccavimus: Numeri XIIII, et sic quodammodo quaerebant Dei benevolentiam propter quod in persona talium dicit sponsa: *Num quem diligit anima mea vidistis,* ad Moysen et Aaron sermonem dirigendo, et quia non responderunt secundum eorum desiderium sed magis ad contrarium, Numeri XIIII: Nolite ascendere: non enim est Deus vobiscum etc., ideo ad dictam petitionem non ponitur hic responsio.

Paululum cum pertransissem eos. Hic consequenter ponuntur quaedam supradictorum declarativa, scilicet, amoris sponsi et sponsae, et primo ponitur huius amoris reformatio, secundo sponsae commendatio, ibi: *Quae est ista.* Circa primum dicit sponsa: *Paululum cum pertransissem eos* scilicet Moysen et Aaron, de quibus fit sermo immediate praecedens. *Inveni quem diligit anima mea,* quia mortuis Aaron et Moyse et tota illa generatione quae exierat de Aegypto a XX annis et supra ut praedictum est, populus Israel invenit Deum propitium sub Iosue duce qui mirabiliter Iordanem transivit et potenter adversarios devicit. *Tenui eum nec dimittam,* quia toto tempore Iosue populus non recessit a Dei servitate, Iosue ultimum. *Donec introducam illum in domum matris meae, et in cubiculum genitricis meae,* id est, donec figam eius tabernaculum in Sylo, Iosue XVIII. Ibi enim habuit primum tabernaculum Domini stabilem mansionem, ut dictum fuit super librum Iosue et I Reg. Dicitur autem illud tabernaculum in quo Deus specialiter habitabat domus matris et genitricis sponsae pro populo Israel qui tunc erat, quia de oblationibus parentum eius factum fuerat in deserto, Exo. XXXV. Et quia quies populi in servitute Dei erat desideranda, ideo subditur:

Adiuro vos filiae Hierusalem, et exponatur ut supra praecedenti ca. *Ne suscitetis neque evigilare faciatis dilectam donec ipsa velit,* id est, ne declinetis ad idolatriam per quam interrumpitur quies ista, contrarium tamen fecerunt post mortem Iosue, ut patet libro Iudicum, ut dicetur postea.

the people were penitent about their rebellion, and said, "We are ready to go up to the place, of which the Lord hath spoken: for we have sinned," Numbers 14 [40], and thus in some way they sought God's blessing, the bride therefore says in the person of them, *Have you seen him, whom my soul loveth?*, directing her question to Moses and Aaron. But because Moses and Aaron did not reply the way that the people wanted, but rather to the contrary, in Numbers 14 [42]: "Go not up, for the Lord is not with you," therefore no response is given here to the people's request.

[Ch. 3:4] *When I had a little passed by them.* Now come the declarations of the love between the groom and bride mentioned earlier. First comes the change which took place in this love, secondly the praise of the bride, beginning at the words *Who is she* [ch. 3:6]? Pertaining to the first the bride says, *When I had a little passed by them,* namely, Moses and Aaron, referred to in the immediately preceding statement, *I found him whom my soul loveth,* because at the deaths of Aaron and Moses and the deaths of the whole generation which made the exodus from Egypt, twenty years of age and older, as I explained before, the Israelites found God to be gracious. Under their leader Joshua they miraculously crossed the Jordan and decisively conquered their adversaries. *I held him: and I will not let him go,* because during the entire time of Joshua's leadership the people did not cease serving God, Joshua 24 [31], *till I bring him into my mother's house, and into the chamber of her that bore me,* that is, till I build his tabernacle in Shiloh, Joshua 18 [1]. For there, for the first time, the tabernacle of the Lord had a permanent home, as I explained in the books of Joshua and 1 Kings. Besides this, the tabernacle in which God dwelt in a special way is called the mother's house, and the chamber of her who bore the bride. This is a reference to the Israelites who were then living, because of the offering which their parents had made in the desert, Exodus 35. Because it was desirable that the people serve God in peace and quiet, the text adds:

[Ch. 3:5] *I adjure you, O daughters of Jerusalem,* which should be understood as I explained earlier, *that you stir not up, nor awake my beloved, till she please,* that is, do not turn to idolatry by which the quiet service of God is disrupted. However, after the death of Joshua, the people did that anyway, as one can plainly see in the Book of Judges, and as I will explain later.

Quae est ista. Hic consequenter ponitur sponsae commendatio, et primo haec commendatio ponitur sub parabola mulieris virtuosae, et secundo sub parabola mulieris speciosae, ca. sequenti. Prima in duas, quia primo ponitur dicta commendatio, secundo concluditur intenta conclusio, ibi: *Egredimini.* Prima adhuc in tres, quia primo commendatur de sacrificiorum oblatione, secundo de castrorum dispositione, ibi: *En lectulum,* tertio de tabernaculi compositione, ibi: *Ferculum.* Circa primum sciendum quod post oblationem sacrificiorum in altari holocaustorum, quod erat sub divo, sacerdotes offerebant thymiama in altari incensi quod erat in tabernaculo, et tunc erant sacrificia consummata, ut habetur Heb. IX, et quantum ad hoc dicit: *Quae est ista,* id est, quam placida in conspectu Dei. *Quae ascendit per desertum,* tendebat enim ad terram promissionis quae altior est illo deserto. *Sicut virgula fumi ex aromatibus* etc., quod dicitur propter thymiama compositum ex pluribus aromaticis rebus, Exo. XXX, et designabat devotionem populi per quam merebatur ad terram promissionis introduci.

En lectulum. Hic consequenter commendatur de castrorum dispositione quae optime disponebantur circa tabernaculum, ut plenius dixi Numeri III. Tres enim tribus erant in parte orientali, et tres in occidentali et aliae sex in parte aquilonari et meridionali, et hoc est quod dicitur: *En lectulum Salomonis,* id est, tabernaculum foederis, quod dicitur Dei lectulus supra I ca., qui Deus nomine Salomonis intelligitur in hoc libro ut dictum est supra I ca. *Sexaginta fortes,* id est, sexagesies X milia, quae faciunt sexcenta milia pugnatorum, qui excubabant circa tabernaculum, Numeri II, et adhuc erant tria milia d. 1. sed non computantur hic, quia Scriptura frequenter tales minutias omittit. Ponitur autem hic unus fortis ad designandum X milia, quia per LX fortes sexagesies X milia intelliguntur, ut dictum est, eo modo loquendi quo dicitur de David, II Reg. XVIII: Tu unus pro X milibus computaris. *Ex fortissimis Is-*

[Ch. 3:6] *Who is she?* We now have the groom's praise of the bride. First this praise is described by using a parable of a virtuous woman. Secondly, it is described by using a parable of a beautiful woman, in the next chapter. The first praise is divided into two parts: First we have the praise itself. Secondly, we have the intended conclusion, beginning at the words, *Go forth* [ch. 3:11]. The first of these two parts is further divided into three subparts: First the offering of sacrifices is praised. Secondly, the layout of the camps is praised, beginning at the words, *Surrounded the bed* [ch. 3:7]. Thirdly, the construction of the tabernacle is praised, beginning at the words, *A litter* [ch. 3:9]. About the first of these three subparts one must understand that after the offering of sacrifices on the altar of burnt offerings, which was out under the open sky, the priests offered thyme on the altar of incense, which was in the tabernacle, and then the sacrifices were completed, as we find out in Hebrews 9. Concerning this the groom says, *Who is she?*, that is, how pleasing she is in God's sight, *[she] who goeth up by the desert,* for she was on her way to the Promised Land which is at a higher elevation than the desert, *as a pillar of smoke of aromatical spices, [of myrrh, and frankincense, and of all the powders of the perfumer].* This is said because thyme is composed of many fragrant ingredients, Exodus 30 [35]. This statement signified the devotion of the people by which they merited their being led into the Promised Land.

[Ch. 3:7] *[Threescore valiant ones] surrounded the bed.* Next there is praise for the layout of the camps, which were arranged in a very orderly way around the tabernacle, as I explained more fully in my comments on Numbers 3. Three tribes were to the east, three to the west, and the other six to the north and south. About these tribes the text says: *[They] surrounded the bed of Solomon,* that is, the tabernacle of the covenant, which was called God's bed above in chapter one. It is God who is understood by the name of Solomon in this book, as I explained above in chapter one. *Threescore valiant ones,* that is, 600,000, which means 600,000 soldiers, who camped around the tabernacle, Numbers 2 [32]. In addition there were 3,550 men, but they are not counted here, because Scripture frequently omits such small details. Besides this, one valiant man here signifies 10,000, because by threescore valiant men, 600,000 are signified, as I explained. This same way of speaking is used in connection with David in 2 Kings 18 [3]: "For thou alone art accounted for 10,000." *Of the most*

rael. Hoc dicitur ad excludendum mulieres et parvulos et debiles ex senectute qui non procedebant ad bella, qui sunt

Omnes tenentes gladios etc. quia erant prompti et parati ad pugnandum contra inimicos. *Propter timores nocturnos,* id est, propter subitum adventum adversariorum qui solent magis irruere de nocte.

Ferculum. Hic tertio commendatur de tabernaculi compositione, ad cuius constructionem obtulit populus donaria mente devota atque promptissima, Exo. XXXV, quia tamen hoc fuit ad mandatum Dei qui praecepit fieri tabernaculum fidei, ideo dicitur: *Ferculum fecit sibi Rex Salomon,* id est, ipse Deus ad cultum suum fecit fieri tabernaculum. Quod dicitur hic ferculum a fero fers quasi ferculum quia portabatur per Levitas de loco ad locum, ut patet Numeri IIII, unde in Hebraeo sic habetur: *Papilionem fecit sibi Rex Salomon.* Est autem *papilio* domus portabilis *de lignis Libani.* Dicit enim Rabbi Salomon quod Iacob antequam descenderet in Aegyptum vidit in spiritu filios suos inde postea exituros et tabernaculum Deo facturos in deserto ubi non habentur ligna sethim, de quibus tamen factae sunt tabulae tabernaculi et vectes et archa et plura alia, propter quod portavit secum in Aegyptum semina et radices arborum ad opus illud necessariarum de Monte Libani qui est in terra Chanaan, et hoc modo tabernaculum dicitur factum *de lignis Libani.* Si quis autem dictum Rabbi Salomon non recipiat, licet non videatur aliquid absurdum includere, potest dicere: *De lignis Libani,* id est, de lignis similibus illis quae crescunt in Libano.

Columnas eius fecit argenteas, quia intra taber-naculum erant quatuor columnae quarum bases erant argenteae, et in illis columnis pendebat velum dividens sanctum et sanctum sanctorum, et ideo dicuntur argenteae a base quae sustinet totum residuum, Exo. XXVI. *Reclinatorium,* id est, propitiatorium quod erat quasi sedes Dei. *Aureum,* quia totum de auro purissimo, Exo. XXV. *Ascensum*

valiant of Israel. This is stated to exclude women and children and those who were weak with age, that is, those who do not go off to war, and to include those who are

[Ch. 3:8] *All holding swords, [and most expert in war: every man's sword upon his thigh],* because they were ready and prepared for fighting against their enemies, *because of fears in the night,* that is, because of the sudden approach of their adversaries who customarily attacked by night.

[Ch. 3:9] *A litter.* Thirdly, the construction of the tabernacle, for which the people offered gifts with a most ready and devout mind, is praised. But, since the construction was done at the command of God, who ordered that this tabernacle be built, the text therefore says, *King Solomon hath made him a litter,* that is, God himself caused the tabernacle to be built for his own worship. What is here called a "litter" [*ferculum*] comes from *fero fers* [which means "I carry," "you carry," etc.]. A "litter," then, was something "carried" by the Levites from place to place, as Numbers 4 clearly shows. The Hebrew word [translated into Latin as *ferculum*] could also be translated as *papilio,* that is, *King Solomon hath made him a papilio.* A *papilio* would be a portable house made *of wood from Lebanon.* Rabbi Solomon says that Jacob, before he went down to Egypt, had a vision of his sons after they had made their exodus from Egypt, and after they had built the tabernacle of God in the desert, where they did not have setim wood. Yet it was from that wood that the boards of the tabernacle, and the poles, the arches, and many other things were built. Therefore Jacob carried with him into Egypt the seeds and roots of those trees, which were necessary for that construction, from Mt. Lebanon in the land of Canaan, and in this sense the tabernacle is said to be built from the wood of Lebanon. However, if anyone does not accept Rabbi Solomon's explanation, though it does not seem too far-fetched to mention, he is still able to say, *of the wood of Lebanon,* that is, of wood similar to that which grows in Lebanon.

[Ch. 3:10] *The pillars thereof he made of silver.* Inside the tabernacle there were four pillars, the bases of which were silver, and in front of those pillars hung a veil dividing the holy place from the holy of holies. Therefore the pillars are said to be of silver, since the base holds up all the rest, Exodus 26 [32]. *The seat,* that is, the place of sacrifice, which was, as the Jews called it, the seat of God. *Of gold,* because all was of the purest gold, Exodus 25 [11]. *The going up of*

purpureum. Ascensum hic vocatur velum praedictum, eo quod in columnis erat sursum elevatum, et purpureum eo quod erant ibi varietates purpureae intextae, Exo. XXXVI. *Media caritate constravit,* quia post velum intra sanctum sanctorum super pavimentum erat archa in qua erant tabulae et urna aurea habens manna et virga Aaron quae fronduerat, quae erant divinae caritatis ad populum signa. *Propter filias Hierusalem,* id est, propter personas de populo Israel, quibus Hierusalem metropolis erat futura, pro quarum salute ante propitiatorium fiebant orationes a summo sacerdote.

Egredimini. Hic infertur intenta conclusio, scilicet, quod ex consideratione praedictorum beneficiorum populus attendat dilectionem Dei erga ipsum, et potissime in legis datione per quam populum illum sibi eligit et sibi desponsavit, ideo dicitur: *Egredimini filiae Syon,* de meditatione terrestri et carnali. *Et videte Regem Salomonem,* id est, Deum vobis specialiter factum regem in datione legis, quia modus regis est dare legem subditis. *In diademate,* id est, regia dignitate. *Quo coronavit illum mater sua,* id est, plebs Hebraica quando legem eius suscepit tanquam Domini et regis sui eo modo loquendi quo populus aliquis dicitur coronare aliquem in regem suum quando recipit eum in regem et Dominum, sicut de David dicitur, II Reg. V: Et venerunt universae tribus Israel ad David in Ebron, et sequitur ibidem: Unxeruntque David regem super Israel. Dicitur autem hic plebs Hebraica Dei mater, eo quod nasciturus erat de ea secundum carnem per Virginem Mariam, Math. I. *In die desponsationis eius,* id est, tempore dationis legis in quo desponsavit sibi plebem illam, ut dictum est. *Et in die laetitiae cordis eius,* quia Deo fuit placitum verbum populi dicentis, Exo. XXIIII: Omnia verba quae locutus est faciemus.

Cap. IIII.

Quam pulchra es. Hic consequenter commendatur sponsa sub parabola mulieris speciosae, et primo ponetur parabola, secundo exponetur. Quantum ad primum dicitur: *Quam pulchra es,* id est, valde pulchra. *Oculi tui columbarum,* id est, simplicis aspectus, quod multum facit ad gratiositatem mulieris. *Absque eo quod intrinsecus latet,* id est, pulchra membrorum dispositione sub vestibus latente.

purple. Here the above-mentioned veil is called "the going up," in the sense that it was suspended in front of the pillars, and it is described as "purple" in the sense that there were varieties of purple embroidered in it, Exodus 36 [35]. *The midst he covered with charity,* because behind the veil, inside the holy of holies, on the pavement, stood the ark, in which were kept the tablets of the Law, a golden urn containing manna, and the rod of Aaron which had blossomed, all of which were signs of God's love for the people. *For the daughters of Jerusalem,* that is, the tabernacle was made for the Israelites, for whom the city of Jerusalem lay in the future, and for whose welfare, in front of the altar of sacrifice, the high priest offered prayers.

[Ch. 3:11] *Go forth.* Here now is the intended conclusion. After the people gave proper consideration to the above-mentioned blessings, above all the giving of the Law by which God chose them for himself and betrothed them to himself, they gave their full attention to God's love for them. Therefore the text says, *Go forth, ye daughters of Sion,* from thinking about earthly and fleshly matters, *and see King Solomon,* that is, God who became king for you in a special way by giving the Law, because it is in the nature of a king to give laws to his subjects. *In the diadem,* that is, in royal dignity, *wherewith his mother crowned him,* that is, when the Hebrews received God's Law as if from their Lord and King, as it is often said that people crown someone as their king, when they accept him as their lord and king. David is spoken about like this in 2 Kings 5 [1]: "Then all the tribes of Israel came to David in Hebron," and that passage continues [ch. 5:3]: "And they anointed David to be king over Israel." Besides this, the Hebrews are called here the mother of God in the sense that God was to be born from them according to the flesh by means of the Virgin Mary, Matthew 1. *In the day of his espousals,* that is, at the time of the giving of the Law by which he espoused that nation to himself, as I already explained, *and in the day of the joy of his heart,* because God was pleased when the people said, Exodus 24 [7]: "All things that the Lord hath spoken we will do."

[Ch. 4:1] *How beautiful art thou.* Next the bride is praised by using the parable of a beautiful woman. First comes the parable, then it is explained. About the parable itself the text says, *How beautiful art thou,* that is, you are very beautiful. *Thy eyes are doves' eyes,* that is, sincere in appearance, which adds a great deal to a woman's graciousness, *besides what is hid within,* that is, the beautiful alignment of the

Capilli tui sicut greges caprarum etc., id est, ordinate dispositi et compositi. Haec enim similitudo et aliae non sunt in omnibus conditionibus, quia tunc esset identitas, sed aliquando sunt in paucis et aliquando in unica.

Dentes tui sicut greges tonsarum etc., id est, albi et bene ordinati. *Omnes gemellis fetibus,* id est, superiores decenter correspondent inferioribus sicut gemelli ad invicem. *Et sterilis non est inter eas,* id est, non est aliquis dentium fractus vel putrefactus.

Sicut vitta coccinea labia tua, sunt enim labia in parte ubi coniunguntur rubea, quae rubedo iuxta albedinem facit ad decorem. *Et eloquium tuum dulce,* id est, gratum omnibus audientibus ipsum. *Sicut fragmen mali punici,* quod est rubicundum in parte opposita soli. *Ita genae tuae* rubicundae in parte eminentiori iuxta albedinem circumstantem. *Absque eo quod intrinsecus latet,* exponatur ut supra.

Sicut turris David collum tuum, rectum et decenter elevatum, et in hoc tenet similitudo.

Duo ubera tua sicut duo hinnuli capreae gemelli, id est, habentia conformitatem elevationis, non tamen nimiam, sed decentem, inquantum facit ad ostensionem sexus muliebris. Omnia praedicta faciunt ut patet ad corporalem pulchritudinem mulieris. Per hanc autem parabolam intelligitur pulchritudo spiritualis sponsae secundum statum illius temporis, cuius caput dicitur convenienter patriarcha Iacob, alio nomine dictus Israel a quo sicut a capite denominantur Israelitae. Capilli immediate orientes ab hoc capite sunt XII patriarchae. Oculi vero Moyses et Aaron dirigentes populum. Dentes vero bellatores parati ad devorationem adversariorum, unde dixit ille strenus bellator Caleph, Numeri XIIII: Sicut panem possumus eos devorare. Labia vero eloquium dulce proferentia Levitae cantores dicentes divinas laudes. Genae vero rubicundae alii Levitae ministrantes in altari holocaustorum in quo erat ignis continuus. Per guttur autem intelliguntur studiosi in lege, ut dicit Rabbi Salomon propter hoc comparatur turri David munitae clypeis, quia per tale studium habentur arma contra impugnatores legis divinae. Et per talem modum dicit Magister Sententiarum in principio libri sui in

limbs concealed under the clothing. *Thy hair is a flock of goats [which come up from Mt. Galaad],* that is, smoothly combed and set. This comparison and others are not applicable under all circumstances, because not all circumstances are the same. Sometimes the comparisons are apparent in a few circumstances, and sometimes in only one.

[Ch. 4:2] *Thy teeth as flocks of sheep that are shorn [which come up from the washing],* that is, white and straight, *all with twins,* that is, the bigger teeth correspond nicely to the smaller teeth as twins to each other, *and there is none barren among them,* that is, none of the teeth is broken or decayed.

[Ch. 4:3] *Thy lips are as a scarlet lace,* for lips are red where they meet, and their redness next to white skin causes beauty, *and thy speech sweet,* that is, pleasant to all who hear it. *As a piece of pomegranate,* which is red on the side facing the sun, *thy cheeks are,* since they are reddish at the cheekbones in comparison to the white skin which surrounds them, *beside that which lieth hid within,* as I explained above.

[Ch. 4:4] *Thy neck is as the tower of David,* tall and nicely uplifted, and in that way it is similar to a tower.

[Ch. 4:5] *Thy two breasts like two young roes that are twins,* that is, they are the same size, not too large, but well-proportioned, insofar as they show the female sex. All the above-mentioned things clearly contribute to a woman's bodily beauty. However, by means of this parable, one should see the spiritual beauty of the bride, that is, the spiritual beauty of Israel during the Old Testament. The bride's head [that is, Israel's head] is, strictly speaking, the patriarch Jacob. But he is often called Israel, from whom, as their head, the Israelites take their name. The hairs growing out from his head are the twelve patriarchs. The eyes are, actually, Moses and Aaron, who led the people. The teeth stand for the warriors who were prepared to devour their enemies, as that stalwart warrior, Caleb, said in Numbers 14 [9]: "We are able to eat them up as bread." The lips refer to the Levitical cantors, their voices uplifted in song, sweetly singing God's praises. The red cheeks mean the other Levites ministering at the altar of burnt offerings, where a fire burned continually. By the throat the scholars of the Law are referred to, as Rabbi Solomon says. Just as David may be compared to a tower fortified with shields, so these scholars, by their study, were armed against those who might attack God's Law. The Master of the Sentences [Peter Lombard] speaks simi-

quo ponuntur sententiae studiosorum in divina lege: Fidem nostram
adversus carnalium hominum errores Daviticae turris clypeis munire
vel potius munitam ostendere studuimus. Duo ubera sunt duae tabulae testimonii, ex quibus suggitur lac sacrae scientiae et devotionis.

Donec aspiret dies, scilicet, Novi Testamenti de quo dicit Apostolus,
Ro. XIII: Nox praecessit dies autem appropinquavit, unde dicitur
Luce. XVI: Lex et prophetae usquam ad Iohannem, in quo incepit
dies Novi Testamenti. *Et inclinentur umbrae,* quia in Novo Testa-
mento cessant figurae adveniente veritate, cuius quodammodo erant
umbrae.

Vadam ad montem. Postquam Salomon descripsit mutuum
amorem sponsi et sponsae secundum statum egressus de Aegypto et
processus in deserto, hic consequenter idem facit secundum statum
accessus ad terminum, scilicet, ad terram sanctam. Et dividitur in
duas partes, quia primo describitur quantum ad ingressum terrae,
secundo quantum ad statum ipsius possessae, capitulo sequenti. Circa
primum excitatur sponsa ex duobus ad ingressum terrae, secundum
ponitur ibi: *Hortus conclusus.* Primum autem excitativum est amor
sponsi et sponsae qui facit eos concorditur ambulare, propter quod
dicit sponsus: *Vadam ad montem* etc., id est, ad terram Iudaeae quae
est montuosa et in qua crescunt aromatica inter quae est myrrha
quasi diceret sponsae, hoc debet te excitare ad veniendum illuc, quia
consors ero et dux viae tuae hoc enim dixit Dominus Iosue I: Sicut
fui cum Moyse, ita ero tecum, non dimittam te nec derelinquam, tu
enim sorte divides populo huic terram, pro qua iuravi patribus tuis,
et ut magis excitet eam commendat eam dicens.

Tota pulchra es amica mea, quia interfectis illis imminente Moysi
morte qui peccaverant in peccato Phegor, Nume. XXV, populus
remansit sine notabili macula peccati sub Iosue.

Veni de Libano. Non est hic Libanus nomen montis in Iudaea
existentis, sed alterius loci ultra Iordanem, unde filii Israel venerunt

larly in his First Book [of *Sentences*] which contains the sentences of scholars who study God's Law: "We study our faith in order to fortify ourselves against the errors of sinful men with the shields of the tower of David, or rather, we study to show how we are fortified." The two breasts are the two tablets of the Law, from which one draws the milk of sacred knowledge and devotion.

[Ch. 4:6a] *Till the day break,* namely, the period of the New Testament about which the Apostle says in Romans 13 [12], "The night is passed, and the day is at hand." Likewise, Luke 16 [16] says, "The law and the prophets were until John," with whom the day of the New Testament dawned. *And the shadows retire,* because in the New Testament the figures cease when the Truth comes, whose shadows in a certain sense they were.

[Ch. 4:6b] *I will go to the mountain.* Now that Solomon has described the love between the groom and bride in terms of the exodus from Egypt and the journey in the desert, he next does the same thing in terms of the ascent to the goal of the journey, namely, the Holy Land. This is divided into two parts: First the entry into the Holy Land, and secondly, how it was captured, which is covered in the next chapter. Pertaining to the entry into the Holy Land, the bride is made eager by two things. The second begins at the words, *A garden enclosed* [ch. 4:12]. But first the love between the groom and bride is built up, which causes them to walk in harmony. The groom says, *I will go to the mountain [of myrrh],* that is, to the land of Judea, which is mountainous and from which pleasant odors arise, one of which is myrrh, as if the groom said to the bride, You ought to be eager to go there, since I will be your companion and leader on your journey. As the Lord said in Joshua 1 [5]: "As I have been with Moses, so will I be with thee. I will not leave thee, nor forsake thee. [6] For thou shalt divide the land by lot for this people, concerning which I swore to your fathers, [that I would deliver it to them]." To make the bride all the more eager, the groom praises her, saying:

[Ch. 4:7] *Thou art all fair, O my love,* because, after those who had joined in the sin of Baal Phegor were slain, Numbers 25, and after Moses had died, the people lived without any special stain of sin under Joshua's leadership.

[Ch. 4:8] *Come from Libanus.* Here Libanus [that is, Lebanon] is not the name of the mountain which rises in Judea, but rather an elevation above the Jordan River, where the children of Israel entered

in Iudaeam. Frequenter enim diversa loca eisdem nominibus nominantur. Et dicitur hic ter *veni,* ad maiorem excitationem, sicut Hiere. XXII: Terra terra terra audi verbum Domini. *Coronaberis de capite Amana* etc. In Hebraeo habetur: *Respicies de capite Amana.* Sunt enim Amana, Sanir, et Hermon nomina montium ultra Iordanem existentium unde videtur terra Iudaeae, et ideo populus Israel illuc veniens aspiciebat terram sibi promissam gaudens propter eius pulchritudinem, et forte imposuerunt sibi serta vel coronas in signum exultationis, secundum quod habet translatio nostra: *Coronaberis de capite Amana* etc., id est, videbis terram tibi promissam de locis istis. *De cubilibus leonum* etc., in montibus enim illis erant cubilia leonum et pardorum, non tamen nocuerunt filiis Israel, sicut nec serpentes horribiles in deserto existentes, per quod filii Israel transierunt, Deut. VIII.

Vulnerasti cor meum. Modus est loquendi amantium ad expressionem amoris. *In uno oculorum tuorum,* id est, in Moyse qui supradictus est unus oculus sponsae, qui fuit Deo valde amabilis et propter eum fuit Deus populo favorabilis. *Et in uno crine colli tui,* id est, in Ioseph qui fuit Deo valde acceptus, et fuit unus de capillis sponsae seu crinibus ut dictum est supra.

Quam pulchrae sunt mammae tuae etc., exponatur ut supra de uberibus sponsae, quae dicuntur hic. *Pulchriora vino,* propter pulchritudinem et mundiciam legis contentae in tabulis.

Favus distillans labia tua sponsa mel et lac sub lingua tua. Hoc dicitur de orationibus devotis summi pontificis et cantorum quae fiebant in persona totius Ecclesiae. *Et odor vestimentorum tuorum sicut odor thuris.* Hoc dicitur pro unguento odorifero quo unctum fuit tabernaculum et omnia eius utensilia, Exo. XXX. Et dicuntur vestes sponsae, quia tabernaculum erat in magnum decorem et ornatum totius populi.

Hortus conclusus. Hic ponitur secundum incitativum ad terrae promissionis ingressum, quod est fertilitas terrae et eius amenitas, et

Judea. For frequently different places have the same name. The text repeats the word "come" three times in order to heighten the bride's eagerness, just as it does in Jeremiah 22 [9]: "O earth, earth, earth, hear the word of the Lord." *Thou shalt be crowned from the top of Amana, [from the top of Sanir and Hermon].* The Hebrew text says, *Thou shalt look from the top of Amana.* Amana, Sanir, and Hermon are the names of mountains rising above the Jordan River from which one can see the land of Judea. The Israelites, upon arriving there, looked out over the Promised Land, and rejoiced because of its beauty. As they did so, they placed wreaths or crowns on their heads as a sign of great happiness. This is what is reflected in our [Latin] translation: *Thou shalt be crowned from the top of Amana* etc., that is, [with crowns on your head] you will look upon the Promised Land from these heights, *from the dens of the lions [from the mountains of the leopards],* since the dens of lions and leopards were found in those mountains. However, these beasts did not harm the children of Israel, nor did the fearsome snakes which lived in the desert through which the Israelites traveled, as mentioned in Deuteronomy 8 [5].

[Ch. 4:9] *Thou hast wounded my heart.* This is the way lovers speak to express their love. *With one of thy eyes,* that is, with Moses, who was called earlier an eye of the bride. He was very lovely in the sight of God, and God dealt favorably with the people because of him. *And with one hair of thy neck,* that is, with Joseph, who was also very acceptable to God. He was one of the hairs of the bride, as I explained earlier.

[Ch. 4:10] *How beautiful are thy breasts* etc. Breasts should be understood as I explained earlier. Here they are said to be *more beautiful than wine,* because of the beauty and elegance contained in the tablets of the Law.

[Ch. 4:11] *Thy lips, my spouse, are as a dropping honeycomb, honey and milk are under thy tongue.* This refers to the prayers of the high priest and the cantors which were devoutly offered on behalf of the whole church. *And the smell of thy garments, as the smell of frankincense.* This refers to the sweet-smelling ointment which was poured over the tabernacle and all its utensils, Exodus 30. The ointment is said to be the garments of the bride because the tabernacle was very beautiful and the adornment of all the people.

[Ch. 4:12] *A garden enclosed.* Here now is the second inducement to enter the Promised Land, namely, the fertility of the land

coniungatur sic littera: O *soror mea sponsa,* id est, O Ecclesia Israel, quae dicitur sponsa Dei, eo quod desponsavit eam per legem in Monte Synai, et soror, quantum humanitatem erat accepturus de gente illa. *Hortus conclusus,* supple est terra tibi promissa. Hortus propter eius fecunditatem. *Conclusus* propter eius fortitudinem, quia ab occidente clauditur Mari Mediterraneo, ab oriente Iordane Fluvio, ab aquilone Monte Libani, a meridie deserto Aegypti, qui non potest de facili transiri. *Fons signatus.* Ponitur hic fons in singulari pro fontibus in plurali, sicut frequenter alibi fit in Scriptura. Habet enim illa terra multos fontes ita limpidos ac si essent sigulati ne bestia vel homo posset aquam turbare.

Emissiones tuae paradisus, id est, rivuli inde de fluentes reddunt terram amoenam ad modum paradisi, unde de quadam parte illius terrae dicitur Gen. XIII: Elevatis itaque Loth oculis vidit omnem circa regionem Iordanis, quae universa irrigabatur sicut paradisus Domini etc. *Malorum punicorum,* id est, malorum granatorum quae crescunt in illa terra cum multis aliis arboribus fructiferis. *Cypri cum nardo.* Est autem hic cypri nominativi casus et plurale huius nominis cyprus quae est arbor aromatica, et etiam crescit in vincis Engaddi, ut dictum est supra, c. I. Similiter *nardus* est planta aromatica.

Et crocus, herba aromatica Gallis saffren. *Fistula.* Herba est producens cannas quarum succus per decoctionem fit zucara. *Et cinamomum.* Arbor est aromaticacuius cortex canele Gallice dicitur. *Cum universis lignis Libani.* Est enim Mons Libani in extremitate terrae promissionis versus aquilonem in quo crescunt cedri et multa alia ligna preciosa. *Myrrha et aloe.* Est autem aloe arbor aromatica, cuius lignum est valde odoriferum, et contritum valet ad medicinas et unguenta, ideo subditur: *Cum omnibus primis,* id est, praecipuis *unguentis.* Haec omnia dicuntur ad terrae promissionis commendationem in qua talia oriuntur, ad cuius commedationem adhuc subditur:

Fons hortorum. Hoc dicitur propter Iordanem Fluvium qui currit secundum longitudinem terrae promissionis eam irrigans in multis

and its pleasantness. The text continues, *O my sister, my spouse,* that is, O Church of Israel, which is called God's "spouse" in the sense that God espoused her by giving the Law on Mt. Sinai, and which is called God's "sister" when one considers the human nature of that nation. *A garden enclosed.* Inviting is the land promised to you, a "garden" because of its productivity, and "enclosed" because of its protection. For on the west it was bordered by the Mediterranean Sea, on the east by the Jordan River, on the north by Mt. Lebanon, and on the south by the Egyptian desert, which cannot be easily crossed. *A fountain sealed up.* Here the singular ("fountain") is used for the plural ("fountains"), as Scripture frequently does elsewhere. For the land has many fountains so clear that a person might think they were sealed off, so that neither animal nor man could muddy the water.

[Ch. 4:13] *Thy plants are a paradise,* that is, rivers flowing through the land make it as pleasant as Paradise. That is why Genesis 13 [10] says about one particular area of that land, "And Lot, lifting up his eyes, saw all the country about the Jordan, which was watered throughout . . . as the paradise of the Lord" etc. *Of pomegranates,* that is, a paradise of pomegranate trees which grow in that land along with many other fruit-bearing trees. *Cypress with spikenard.* Here "cypress" [*cypri*] is the [Latin] nominative plural case of the [Latin] nominative singular "cypress" [*cyprus*], which is an aromatic tree that grows in the vicinity of Engaddi, as I explained above in chapter one. Similarly, *spikenard* is an aromatic plant.

[Ch. 4:14] *And crocus,* another aromatic plant, the French *safran.* *Sweet cane.* This is an herb which grows in the form of canes. The juice of these canes, when boiled down, forms sugar. *And cinnamon.* This is another aromatic tree, whose bark is called *cannelle* in French. *With all the trees of Libanus.* Recall that Mt. Lebanon is in the extreme north of the Promised Land where cedars and many other valuable trees grow. *Myrrh and aloes.* An aloe is also an aromatic tree, whose wood is very sweet smelling, and, when ground to a powder, is valuable for making medicines and ointments. To this the text adds, *With all the chief perfumes,* that is, outstanding *ointments.* All these things are enumerated in order to praise the Promised Land, where such things are found, and to praise it further the text adds:

[Ch. 4:15] *The fountain of gardens.* This is added because the Jordan River flows the length of the Promised Land, watering it all

locis, ideo subditur: Fons hortorum, et accipitur hic fons in singulari pro fontibus in plurali, sicut dicitur: Sillogismus est oratio, id est, congeries orationum, quia Iordanis ex duobus fontibus oritur, quorum unus vocatur Ior, alius Dan, qui simul iuncti Iordanis nomen efficiunt, ut dicit Hieronymus super Math., et patet in descriptione terrae sanctae. *Puteus aquarum,* quia Iordanis abundat in aquis, eo modo loquendi quo aliquis abundans in pecuniis dicitur puteus pecuniarum. *Viventium,* dicuntur enim proprie vivere illa qui habent in se principium sui motus, ut animalia et etiam plantae, inquantum habent in se principium sui motus secundum augmentum et decrementum. Et ad similitudinem huius dicuntur aquae viventes quae scaturiunt ex fontibus, quales sunt aquae Iordanis. Aquae vero cisternales dicuntur mortuae. *Quae fluunt impetu de Libano,* Iordanis enim oritur ex fontibus praedictis ad radices Montis Libani, ut dicit Hieronymus super Math.

Surge aquilo et veni auster etc., quia ad flatum ventorum oppositarum partium fluunt guttae aromaticae de arboribus aromaticis huius terrae quae colliguntur ab incolis eo quod sunt preciosae. Haec omnia praedicta sunt de commendatione terrae promissae ad excitandum desiderium sponsae.

Cap. V.

Veniat dilectus meus. Postquam descripsit Salomon amorem sponsi et sponsae prout respicit ingressum terrae, hic consequenter idem describit prout respicit tempus ipsius possessae, et dividitur in duas partes, quia primo facit hoc secundum tempora Iosue et Iudicum, secundo secundum tempora a David usque ad Christum, ca. sequenti. Circa primum sciendum quod populus Israel illis temporibus aliquando fuit in prosperis, aliquando in adversis, et ideo primo tanguntur prospera, secundo adversa, ibi: *Ego dormio.* Circa primum dicit sponsa: *Veniat dilectus meus in hortum suum,* id est, habitet mecum per condescensionem suae bonitatis in terra mihi concessa quae vocatur hortus Domini, eo quod colebatur ibi. *Ut comedat fructum pomporum suorum,* id est, ut comedere me faciat fructus terrae mihi datae in pace, eo modo loquendi quo dixit Dominus Abrahe Gen. XXII: Nunc

over. Here again, "fountain" in the singular stands for "fountains" in the plural, the same way that a person might say, "A syllogism is a statement," that is, a group of statements. You see, the Jordan arises from two springs, one called "Jor" and the other "Dan." These two, joined together, form the name "Jordan," as Jerome says in his commentary on Matthew. This is clearly seen in the description of the Holy Land. *The well of [living] waters,* because the Jordan abounds in waters, the way that a person might call someone who abounds in wealth a well of wealth. *Living,* for things are correctly said to be "living" if they have within themselves the source of their own motion. This is true of both animals and plants, insofar as they have within themselves the source of their own motion, either increasing or decreasing. Similarly, waters which flow from springs are called "living waters." Such are the waters of Jordan. In contrast, waters which are in cisterns are called "dead waters." *Which run with a strong stream from Libanus,* for the Jordan arises in the above-mentioned springs at the base of Mt. Lebanon, as Jerome says in his commentary on Matthew.

[Ch. 4:16] *Arise, O north wind, and come, O south wind,* etc., because, due to the blowing of the winds from opposite directions, the sweet-smelling drops which come from the trees of this land, and which the inhabitants gather because they are precious, flow. All these things are said in order to praise the Promised Land and thereby arouse the bride's desire for it.

[Ch. 5:1] *Let my beloved come.* Now that Solomon has described the love between the groom and bride in terms of the entrance into the land, he next describes it in terms of its possession. This is divided into two parts. First he does this in terms of the time of Joshua and Judges, secondly in terms of the time from David to Christ in the following chapter. Pertaining to the first of these, you have to understand that the Israelites in those days sometimes lived in prosperity and sometimes in adversity. So the prosperous days are dealt with first, and then the adverse days, at the words *I sleep* [ch. 5:7]. Pertaining to the first of these the bride says, *Let my beloved come into his garden,* that is, let him live with me out of his condescending goodness in the land given to me. It is called the garden of the Lord in the sense that he was living there. *And eat the fruit of his apple trees,* that is, he made me eat in peace the fruit of the land which he gave to me, the same way that the Lord said to Abraham in Genesis 22 [12]:

cognovi quod timeas Dominum, id est, cognoscere feci, vel quia actus et passiones fidelium in Scriptura aliquando attribuuntur ipsi
Deo, Actus IX: Saule, Saule, quid me persequeris, id est, fideles meos,
et ita comestio fructuum terrae attribuitur ipsi Deo, quia populus
eius comedit quando cum Iosue terram intravit, Iosue V: Comederunt
de fructibus terrae defecitque manna, et quia hoc fuit ex dono Dei,
ideo subditur in persona sponsi: *Veni in hortum meum soror mea sponsa,*
habitando ibi in bonorum abundantia, ideo subditur: *Messui myrrham*
meam, id est, preparavi tibi terrae bona. *Comedi,* exponatur ut dictum est. *Favum cum melle meo* etc., per hoc designatur abundantia
mellis vini et lactis in terra illa, propter quod subditur: *Comedite*
amici etc., id est, quamdiu adhaerebitis mihi per amicitiam et latriam,
habebitis omnium bonorum abundantiam, et hoc patet ex decursu
Veteris Testamenti.

 Ego dormio. Hic consequenter ponuntur adversa, populus enim
Israel ex abundantia bonorum temporalium declinavit ad idolatriam,
sicut praedixerat Moyses, Deut. XXXII: Incrassatus est dilectus meus
et recalcitravit, incrassatus impinguatus et dilatatus, dereliquit Deum
factorem suum etc., et ideo Dominus post multam sufferentiam
inflixit poenam debitam, ut sic poena decente reduceretur ad
poenitentiam, propter quod sic proceditur, quia primo ponitur culpa,
secundo poena, ibi: *Dilectus meus,* tertio poenitentia, ibi: *Surrexi.*
Circa primum dicitur in persona Domini: *Ego dormio,* id est, peccata
ad tempus dissimulo, unde communiter dicitur ab hominibus Deus
dormire quando pessimos homines differt punire. *Et cor meum vigilat,*
id est, praevideo tempus debitum punitionis, et subditur in persona
sponsae adulterantis a sponso revocatae: *Vox dilecti mei,* per prophetas
suos et doctores. *Pulsantis,* me ad poenitentiam. *Aperi mihi,* per
consensum boni. *Soror mea amica mea* etc., tempore, scilicet,
praeterito tuae innocentiae. *Quia caput meum est plenum rore,* per

"Now I know that thou fearest God," that is, I made you recognize me as God; or the way that the actions and passions of the faithful in Scripture sometimes are attributed to God himself, as in Acts 9 [4]: "Saul, Saul, why persecutest thou me?", that is, Why do you persecute my faithful people? Thus eating the fruit of the land is attributed to God, in the sense that his people ate the fruit when they entered the land with Josuha, in Joshua 5 [12]: "And the manna ceased after they ate of the fruit of the land." Because this food was a gift of God, the text therefore adds in the person of the groom, *I am come into my garden, O my sister, my spouse,* by living there amid the abundance of good things. Similarly, the text also adds, *I have gathered my myrrh,* that is, I have prepared for you the goods of the land. *I have eaten* is explained as I did above. *The honeycomb with my honey, [I have drunk my wine with my milk].* This indicates the abundance of honey, wine, and milk in the land. Because of this the text adds, *Eat, O friends [and drink, and be inebriated, my dearly beloved],* that is, when you cling to me by your affection and worship, you will have an abundance of everything good, and this is clearly shown throughout the Old Testament.

[Ch. 5:2] *I sleep.* Now come the adversities. For the Israelites turned away from the abundance of earthly blessings to idolatry, just as Moses had predicted in Deuteronomy 32 [15]: "The beloved grew fat, and kicked: he grew fat, and thick and gross, he forsook God who made him [and departed from God his Savior]." That is why, after showing a great deal of patience, the Lord inflicted on them the punishment which they deserved. Then, in order that the properly given punishment might be reduced to penance, the text goes on as follows: First, the guilt is laid on the Israelites; then the punishment is given, at the words, *My beloved* [ch. 5:4]. Finally, the penance comes at the words *I arose up* [ch. 5:5]. About the first of these the text says, in the person of the Lord, *I sleep,* that is, I temporarily overlook Israel's sins. Thus people commonly say that God is sleeping when he postpones punishing evil men. *And my heart watcheth,* that is, I see in advance the time when punishment is due. The text then adds in the person of the adulterous bride whom the groom calls back from her sin, *The voice of my beloved,* that is, through his prophets and doctors, *knocking,* [that is, calling] me to penance. [The voice says,] *Open to me,* by consenting to do good, *my sister, my love, [my dove, my undefiled],* that is, live righteously as you used to in the past when you

rorem intelligitur parva pluvia, per guttas noctium magna. Ros enim
et pluvia differunt secundum paucitatem et multiplicitatem materiae,
I Metaurorum. Et loquitur hic Deus secundum modum sponsi
reconciliationem suae sponsae desiderantis, et non retardatur ab hoc
ex importunitate temporis. Et subditur responsio sponsae malae
reconciliationem recusantis, cum dicitur:

Expoliavi me tunica mea, id est, dimisi cultum divinum
consuetum, iam diu est, sicut patet in processu libri Iudicum. Modus
enim vivendi consuetus alicuius vulgariter dicitur tunica eius. *Quo-
modo induar illa,* quia per admonitiones prophetarum nolebat populus
reverti ad cultum divinum. *Lavi pedes meos* etc. Hoc dicitur secundum estimationem idolatrantis populi, qui cultum Dei reputabat
immundum et cultum idoli mundum. Et sic exponit Rabbi Salomon.

Dilectus meus, quia per culpae dissimulationem Deus adhibet
poenam, ideo dicit sponsa: *Dilectus meus misit manum suam,* id est,
manum suae iusticiae ad puniendum me. *Per foramen.* Prosequitur
parabolam sponsi irati contra sponsam apertionem ostii sibi
denegantem, qui per fenestram vel aliquam aperturam infert bacu-
lum ad percutiendum eam. *Et venter meus intremuit ad tactum eius,*
quia populus a Deo percussus concipiebat timorem eius, ut patet
libro Iudicum in pluribus locis.

Surrexi. Hic consequenter poena decente subditur poenitentia.
Et dividitur in duas partes, quia primo per poenitentiam quaeritur
sponsi reconciliatio, secundo ponitur pulchritudinis eius descriptio,
ibi: *Qualis est.* Circa primum dicit sponsa: *Surrexi ut aperirem dilecto
meo,* quaerens ei reconciliari et sic a poena liberari. *Manus meae
distillaverunt myrrham,* id est, applicavi me ad opera poenitentiae
quae designantur per amaritudinem myrrhae.

Pessulum ostii mei aperui etc. Pessulum est ostiolum in magna
porta, et per hoc designatur quod poenitentia in principio est

were innocent. *For my head is full of dew [and my locks of the drops of the nights]*. By "dew" one should understand light showers. By "drops" one should understand heavy rainstorms during the nights. For dew and storms differ according to the amount of their matter, [as Aristotle says in Book] I of his *Meteorology*. God speaks here the way a groom would, who desires reconciliation with his bride, and he is not kept from doing this just because the time might not be suitable. The sinful bride, who refuses reconciliation, responds with:

[Ch. 5:3] *I have put off my garment,* that is, I have ended my customary worship of God. In fact, she had stopped worshiping for a long time already, as is clear from the way things are presented in the Book of Judges. For someone's accustomed way of living is commonly called his garment. *How shall I put it on?,* because, in spite of the admonitions of the prophets, the people refused to return to their worship of God. *I have washed my feet, [how shall I defile them?]*. This is said in accordance with the way these idolatrous people viewed things, for they considered the worship of God to be unclean, and the worship of an idol to be clean. This is how Rabbi Solomon explains it.

[Ch. 5:4] *My beloved.* Because the Israelites ignored their guilt, God laid a punishment on them. The bride says, *My beloved put his hand,* that is, the hand of his righteousness in order to punish me, *through the key hole.* God is compared here to a groom who is angry with his bride for refusing to open the door for him, so he brings in, through a window or some other opening, a stick to strike her. *And my bowels were moved at his touch,* because the people, struck by God as the bride in the parable, developed a fear of God, as one can clearly see in the Book of Judges and in many other places in Scripture.

[Ch. 5:5] *I arose up.* With the punishment properly [laid on the Israelites], the penance now follows. This is divided into two parts. First, through penance, reconciliation is sought with the groom. Second, there is a description of his handsomeness, at the words, *What manner of one is [thy beloved]* [ch. 5:9]. Pertaining to the first the bride says, *I arose up to open to my beloved,* seeking to be reconciled to him and thus freed from my punishment. *My hands dropped with myrrh,* that is, I applied myself to works of penance, which the bitterness of myrrh signifies.

[Ch. 5:6] *I opened the bolt of my door [to my beloved]*. A bolt is a little door set into a larger gate, and this signifies that the penance

imperfecta, propter quod subditur: *At ille declinaverat atque transierat,*
quia non statim ad clamorem populi liberabat eum a poena et quia
ex hoc augebatur afflictio, ideo subditur: *Anima mea liquefacta est,*
sicut sagimen in patella, unde de homine dimisso in afflictione dicitur
vulgariter quod frigitur in sagimine suo. *Quaesivi illum* etc. quia sicut
dictum est, Deus non statim liberabat populum, sed dimittebat eum
affligi ab adversariis, ut a Philisteis, Moabitis, et ceteris gentibus circa
terram Iudaeae existentibus, ut patet ex decursu libri Iudicum et I
Reg., ideo subditur:

Invenerunt me custodes etc., id est, principes gentium in circuitu
Iudaeae existentium, quae nominatur hic civitas a Hierusalem
metropoli Iudaeae. *Percusserunt me,* nocumentum inferendo personis.
Tulerunt pallium meum, spoliando me bonis meis, et quia populus
communis propter peccatum idolatriae non erat dignus exaudiri, ideo
convertit se sponsa ad personas mundas ab idolatria, quia semper in
populo Israel fuerunt aliquae personae tales quantumcumque populus
communis, vel etiam principes ad idolatriam declinarent,unde III
Reg. XIX dicit Dominus ad Heliam: Derelinquam mihi in Israel sex
milia virorum quorum genua non sunt curvata ante Baal. Et quia
preces talium sunt exaudibiles, ideo dicit:

Adiuro vos filiae Hierusalem, id est, personae devotae de Israel.
Nec est contra illud quod dictum est supra I ca. quod filiae Hierusalem
significant fragiles populi, quia tam perfectae personae quam
imperfectae sunt de eodem populo, sed supra I ca. imperfectae
dicunter filiae Hierusalem propter fragilitatem sexus. Hic autem
perfectae eodem nomine nominantur ratione devotionis de qua fit
hic mentio quae magis vigere solet in mulieribus, secundum illud
quod canit Ecclesia: Intercede pro devoto femineo sexu. Idem enim
nomen in Sacra Scriptura ex diversis proprietatibus non solum
accipitur pro diversis, sed etiam aliquando pro contrariis, sicut
Deus leo dicitur ratione magnanimitatis Apoc. V, Vicit leo de
tribu Iuda, et diabolus ratione rapacitatis I Petri V, Adversarius
vester diabolus tamquam leo rugiens etc. Dicit igitur: *Adiuro vos,*

was at first imperfect. This is shown by the words, *but he turned aside and was gone,* since God did not free the Israelites immediately from their punishment when they began crying out to him. Since, in this way, their affliction was increased, the text therefore adds, *My soul is melted* like fat in a pan. It is often said of a person who suffers many afflictions, "He is being fried in his own fat." *I sought him [and found him not: I called, and he did not answer me],* because, as I explained, God did not immediately free the people, but subjected them to affliction at the hands of their enemies, for example, the Philistines, the Moabites, and some other nations which bordered Judea. This is clear from the way things are described in the Books of Judges and 1 Kings. Because of this the text adds:

[Ch. 5:7] *The keepers [that go about the city] found me,* that is, the leaders of the nations that surrounded Judea, which is here called a city because Jerusalem is the main city in Judea. *They struck me,* inflicting wounds on me. *[The keepers of the walls] took away my veil [from me],* by stripping me of my goods. Since the common people, due to their sin of idolatry, were not worthy to be heard, she therefore turned to the people who had not committed idolatry, for among the Israelites there were always a certain number of common people, or even leaders, who turned to idolatry. That is why in 3 Kings 19 [18] the Lord says to Elijah: "And I will leave me six thousand men in Israel, whose knees have not bowed before Baal." Since the prayers of faithful people like these are heard, the bride therefore says:

[Ch. 5:8] *I adjure you, O daughters of Jerusalem,* that is, you Israelites who are spiritually strong. This is not a contradiction of what was said above in chapter one, that the daughters of Jerusalem signify the spiritually weak Israelites, because there were as many spiritually strong as weak Israelites. Above, in chapter one, the daughters of Jerusalem were said to be weak because of the weakness of women. Here, however, they are called strong because of their devotion to God, which often thrives more among women than men. This is why the church sings, "Pray for the devoutness of women." Recall that Sacred Scripture uses the same word in various connotations, even contrary ones. That is why God can be called a lion because of his strength in Apocalypse 5 [5], "Behold the lion of the tribe of Judah," and the devil can also be called a lion because of his ferociousness in 1 Peter 5 [8], "Your adversary the devil, as a roaring lion, [goeth about seeking whom he may devour]." Therefore the bride

id est, per rem sacram deprecor. *Filiae Hierusalem,* id est, devotae personae. *Si inveneritis dilectum meum,* vobis gratiosum in orationibus vestris. *Ut nuncietis ei,* pro me deprecando. *Quia amore langueo,* id est, reconciliari sibi desidero.

Qualis est. Hic consequenter ponitur sponsi descriptio. Et dividitur in duas partes, quia primo circa hoc movetur quaestio, secundo ponitur responsio, ibi: *Dilectus meus.* Circa primum sciendum, quod sicut populus peccator recurrebat ad devotos populi ad habendum orationis suffragium, ita econverso devoti inducebant populum ad cognitionem Dei et ad eius verum cultum, ideo in persona eorum dicitur: *Qualis est dilectus tuus,* id est, utinam attenderes quantum est amabilis et bonus. *Ex dilecto,* id est, prae omnibus diligendus, vel hoc dicitur ad denotandum processionem divinarum personarum, quia Filius procedit a Patre sicut dilectus ex dilecto, et Spiritus Sanctus ab ambobus, ut amor mutuus utriusque. *O pulcherrima mulierum,* id est, aliarum gentium pro tempore desponsationis tuae in susceptione legis divinae ut dictum est supra. *Qualis est dilectus* etc., repetitio est eiusdem ad maiorem excitationem.

Dilectus meus. Hic ponitur sponsae responsio confitendo Dei pulchritudinem et bonitatem: Quia corde creditur ad iusticiam, ore autem fit confessio ad salutem, Ro. X. Et dividitur in duas partes, quia primo ponitur sponsi descriptio, secundo ex hoc oritur quaestio, ibi: *Quo abiit.* Circa primum describitur sponsus sub parabola iuvenis fortis et gratiosi, propter quod primo parabola ponetur, secundo exponetur. Circa primum dicitur: *Dilectus meus candidus et rubicundus,* id est, in colore gratiosus. *Electus ex milibus,* id est, in multis milibus non inveniretur unus talis.

Caput eius aurum optimum, id est, ornatum corona aurea. *Comae eius sicut elatae palmarum,* id est, frondes habentes densitatem foliorum, et per hoc intelligitur multitudo capillorum. *Nigrae quasi*

says, *I adjure you,* that is, in a sacred manner I pray you, *O daughters of Jerusalem,* that is, those of you who are spiritually strong, *if you find my beloved,* thanks to you and your prayers, *that you tell him* pleading for me, *that I languish with love,* that is, I desire to be reconciled with him.

[Ch.5:9] *What manner of one is [thy beloved]?* Next comes the description of the groom. It is divided into two parts. First a question is asked. Then a response is made, at the words, *My beloved* [ch. 5:10]. Pertaining to the question it should be understood that just as the sinful Israelites turned to the devout to have the support of their prayer, so in turn the devout Israelites led the sinful to a recognition of God and to the true worship of him. Therefore in the person of the devout Israelites, the text says, *What manner of one is thy beloved,* that is, O, if only you would turn your attention to God, since he is lovable and good, *of the beloved,* that is, he is more desirable than anyone else. Or perhaps this phrase denotes the procession of the divine persons, since the Son proceeds from the Father—the beloved [Son] from the beloved [Father]—and the Holy Spirit proceeds from both just as love flows from one to the other. *O thou most beautiful among women,* that is, in comparison to other nations, from the time of your engagement to God when you received his holy Law, as I explained earlier. *What manner of one is [thy] beloved [of the beloved].* The same words are repeated in order to arouse still greater desire for God.

[Ch. 5:10] *My beloved.* Now the bride answers her own question, thereby making a confession about the beauty and goodness of God, "For, with the heart, we believe unto justice; but, with the mouth, confession is made unto salvation," Romans 10 [10]. Her answer is divided into two parts. First comes the description of the groom, then a question arises from this, at the words, *Whither is [thy beloved] gone* [ch. 5:17]. Pertaining to the description, the groom is described by using the parable of a strong and well-built young man. First we have the parable, then it is explained. Pertaining to the parable itself, the text says, *My beloved is white and ruddy,* that is, his complexion is favorable, *chosen out of thousands,* that is, there is no one like him among many thousands of young men.

[Ch. 5:11] *His head is as the finest gold,* that is, he is adorned with a gold crown. *His locks as branches of palm trees,* that is, like branches with dense foliage. This refers to the thickness of his hair. *Black as a*

corvus, nigredo capillorum attestatur fortitudini et iuventuti, et quia hic ponitur metaphora iuvenis fortis, dicuntur comae eius nigrae, Dan. VII, ubi describitur Deus sub parabola iudicis in quo decens est senectus et canicies. Dicitur de eo, Antiquus sedit dierum, et subditur: Capilli eius tamquam lana munda, id est, alba.

Oculi eius sicut columbae, id est, habens aspectum simplicem et honestum. *Super rivulos aquarum,* ad se lavandum, ne apparet in eis aliquid immundum. *Quae lacte sunt lotae,* id est, albae ad modum lactis, tales enim columbae sunt gratiosiores aliis, et per hoc notatur gratiositas sponsi in oculis.

Genae illius sicut areolae aromatum. Est autem areola portio terrae bene seminata, unde Ezech. XVII: De areolis germinis sui, quae delectant valde visum quando incipiunt semina pullulare. Dicet enim prophetus quod virides sationes maxime delectant visum et confortant et maxime quando sunt herbae aromaticae. Dicit igitur: *Genae illius sicut areolae aromatum,* id est, sunt ita delectabiles ad videndum sicut areolae seminum aromaticorum pullulantium. *Consitae a pigmentariis,* id est, cultae et ordinatae a bonis cultoribus aromatum quae etiam pigmenta dicuntur. *Labia eius lilia distillantia myrrham primam.* Sic est in Hebraeo, et per hoc designatur mundicia eloquii et gratiositas.

Manus eius tornatiles aureae. In Hebraeo habetur: *Rotae aureae,* per quod designatur quod manus sponsi sunt ornatae annulis aureis qui sunt figurae circularis, ideo subditur: *Plenae hyacinthis,* id est, sapphyris qui sunt hyacinthini coloris, tales enim lapides ponuntur in annulis. *Venter eius eburneus,* id est, albus et politus. *Distinctus sapphyris,* id est, ornatus lapidibus preciosis non immediate super carnem, sed super vestem quae operit ventrem. Sicut enim in vestibus circa collum et manus ad ornatum nobilium nunc ponuntur lapides preciosi, ita etiam tunc temporis circa partes versus ventrem descendentes.

Crura eius columnae marmoreae, id est, fortia ad modum talium columnarum. *Super basas aureas,* id est, super pedes calciatos calciis in superficie de auratis, quales portant nobiles de Hispania. *Species eius ut libani,* id est, forma eius gratiosa sicut libanus quae est arbor aromatica ramosa et valde gratiosa. Libanus enim non est

raven, the blackness of his hair attesting to his strength and youth. His hair is described as black because the metaphor of a strong young man is used here. This is similar to Daniel 7 [9] where God is described with the parable of a judge. There God is fittingly described as old and hoary-haired. The text says, "The Ancient of days sat," and goes on: "And the hair of his head like clean wool," that is, white.

[Ch. 5:12] *His eyes as doves,* that is, his eyes are frank and honest in appearance, *upon brooks of waters,* for washing themselves lest there appear anything unclean in them. *Which are washed with milk,* that is, white as milk. Doves with such eyes are more prized than others. In this way the text denotes how favorable the groom appears in the eyes of the bride.

[Ch. 5:13] *His cheeks are beds of aromatical spices.* The term "bed" is used for ground which is sown and well-tended. For example, Ezekiel 17 [6-7?] speaks about beds which contain a new planting of vines, and when these begin to send out their shoots, they are especially delightful to look at. The prophet says that green fields are a special delight and comfort to see when they contain sweet-smelling herbs. Therefore the text says, *His cheeks are as beds of aromatical spices,* that is, they are as delightful to see as beds of sweet-smelling shoots, *set by the perfumers,* that is, tilled and tended by expert tillers of sweet-smelling spices, which are called perfumes. *His lips are as lilies dropping choice myrrh.* So it is in the Hebrew, and this signifies that he speaks eloquently and graciously.

[Ch. 5:14] *His hands are turned and as of gold.* The Hebrew has *gold wheel,* which means that the groom's hands are adorned with gold rings which are of a circular shape. Therefore the text adds, *Full of hyacinths,* that is, sapphires, which have the color of hyacinths, for rings are often set with such stones. *His stomach as of ivory,* that is, white and smooth, *set with sapphires,* that is adorned with precious stones, not embedded directly in the flesh, but on the clothing which covers the stomach. For then just as now, precious stones were woven into nobles' clothing at the neck and the wrists, and around the stomach, for adornment.

[Ch. 5:15] *His legs as pillars of marble,* that is, strong like marble pillars, *[that are set] upon bases of gold,* that is, his legs rise from his feet on which he wears golden shoes such as Spanish nobles wear. *His form as of Libanus,* that is, his body as finely shaped as a cedar of Lebanon, which has finely shaped, sweet-smelling branches. Note

hic nomen montis prout acceptum est supra in pluribus locis. *Electus ut cedri,* id est, statura eius recta ad modum cedri.

Guttur illius suavissimum, id est, album politum et gratiosum. Et quia omnia praedicta faciunt ad gratiositatem iuvenis, ideo subditur: *Et totus desiderabilis.* Haec autem parabola secundum omnes doctores Hebraicos et Latinos intelligitur de Deo, de quo dicit Gregorius, Moralia XIIII: In Deo qui forma corporis non circumscribitur manus, oculus, et cetera membra sic nominantur, ut ex membrorum vocabulis effectus suae potentiae designentur. Habere namque oculos dicitur, quia cuncta videt, manus quia omnia operatur. Sic ergo de Deo dicitur:

Dilectus meus candidus et rubicundus, id est, benignus iustis, et iratus reprobis, facies enim hominis irati rubescit et exardescit. *Electus ex milibus,* id est, prae omnibus diligendus. In Hebraeo habetur: *Vexillatus in milibus,* id est, habens in exercitu suo multa milia angelorum, Dan. VII: Milia milium ministrabant ei, et decies milies centena milia assistebant ei.

Caput eius aurum optimum, id est, corona aurea decoratum, in qua notatur dignitas regia, qua dicitur Rex regum et Dominus dominantium. *Comae eius,* id est, attributa divina, ut sapientia, bonitas, etc., quia sicut comae inhaerent capiti et adiacent ei, sic attributa sunt idem cum divina essentia, tamen signantur per modum qualitatum sibi adiacentium. *Sicut elatae palmarum,* quia multa sunt. *Nigrae quasi corvus,* quia non senescunt, per nigredinem enim hic intelligitur iuventus ut praedictum est.

Oculi eius sicut columbae, quia uno simplici intuitu videt omnia. *Quae lacte sunt lotae,* quia ex cognitione corvum quae sunt extra se non vilescit intellectus eius, ut dicit commentator Averrois super XII Metaph.: Non enim cognoscit ea per formam extraneam a rebus acceptam, sed per suam essentiam omnia perfecte representantem.

that "Lebanon" here is not the name of the mountain as frequently above. *Excellent as the cedars,* that is, his stature is erect the way cedar trees grow.

[Ch. 5:16] *His throat most sweet,* that is, white, smooth, and finely shaped. Since everything mentioned so far indicates the fine appearance of the young man, the text therefore adds, *and he is all lovely.* Now, this parable, according to all Hebrew and Latin doctors, describes God. For example, Gregory says of God in his *Moralia,* Book 14: "God does not have a bodily form, with an actual hand, or an eye, or any other such member, but he is said to have such members in the sense that they designate his various powers. So God is said to have eyes, because he sees everything; hands, because he controls all things." In this sense, then, the text says of God:

[Ch. 5:10] *My beloved is white and ruddy,* that is, God is kind toward the righteous, and angry toward the condemned, since the face of an angry man glows red, *chosen out of thousands,* that is, God is more desirable than anyone else. The Hebrew has *the standard-bearer among the thousands,* that is, God has an army of many thousands of angels, as it says in Daniel 7 [10]: "Thousands of thousands ministered to Him, and ten thousand times a hundred thousand stood before Him."

[Ch. 5:11] *His head is as the finest gold,* that is, God's head is adorned with a golden crown, which denotes royal dignity, which is why he is called King of kings and Lord of lords. *His locks,* that is, God's divine attributes, such as wisdom, goodness, etc. Just as locks grow on the head and are part of it, so God's attributes are one with his essence. God's attributes are signified by the qualities each one has. The fact that God has many attributes is signified by the phrase, *as branches of palm trees.* The fact that God's attributes do not weaken with age is signified by the phrase, *black as a raven.* Here blackness indicates youth, as I explained above.

[Ch. 5:12] *His eyes as doves,* because with a single glance God sees everything. *Which are washed with milk,* because in comprehending things which are outside himself, his understanding does not diminish, as Averroes says in his commentary on [Aristotle's] *Metaphysics,* Book 12: "For God does not comprehend a particular thing by the outward form which things take, but by his essence reproducing all things perfectly."

Genae illius, sunt virtus attractiva, sicut oculi virtus cognitiva, trahendo enim ad se electos per fidem et amorem incorporat sibi eos, sicut per genas incorporantur materiales cibi, unde dicit Salvator, Ioh. IIII: Ego cibum habeo manducare quem vos nescitis, quod intelligitur ad litteram de Samaritanis, sibi incorporandis per fidem. *Sicut areolae aromatum* etc., quia sicut ex areola aromatum exalat odor bonus reficiens olfactum, ita ex amore divino attrahente recreantur animae bonorum. *Labia eius* sunt virtus reservativa secretorum quibus loquitur sanctis et prophetis ideo subditur. *Lilia distillantia myrrham primam,* quia verba Domini sunt munda et a corruptione peccati preservativa.

Manus eius, sunt eius potentia operativa. *Tornatiles aureae,* vel secundum Hebraeos, *rotae aureae,* per figuram enim circularem annulorum intelligitur perfectio operum divinorum, Deut. XXXII: Dei perfecta sunt opera. *Venter eius,* est occultatio divinorum iudiciorum, unde de homine occulto communiter dicitur quod non potest sciri quid habeat in ventre. *Eburneus.* Est enim ebur frigidum de album, quia consideratio occultationis iudiciorum Dei incutit frigus timoris a peccato retrahentis, Prov. XV: Per timorem Domini recedet omnis a malo, et sic anima candidatur, et desiderio vitae caelestis ornatur, ideo subditur: *Distinctus sapphyris.* Est enim sapphyrus coloris caelestis.

Crura illius, sunt eius virtus qua sustentat omnia. Et *bases aureae,* supposita divina seu personae. *Species eius ut libani, electus ut cedri,* quia pulchritudo eius est summae delectabilis, et altitudo incomprehensibilis.

Gutter illius suavissimum, et totus desiderabilis, quia infinitae bonitatis. *Talis est dilectus* etc., quasi diceret, corde credo et ore confiteor quod istum debeo super omnia diligere.

Quo abiit. Hic ex praedictis oritur quaestio, vere enim poenitentes confitentes sunt adiuvandi erga Deum a personis perfectis, ideo quaeritur in persona eorum: *Quo abiit dilectus tuus,* quasi dicant, parati sumus te iuvare in reconciliatione ad ipsum, ideo subditur: *Et quaeremus* etc. Ista tamen littera: *Quo abiit* etc., referenda est ad tem-

[Ch. 5:13] *His cheeks* are God's power to attract, just as his eyes are his power to comprehend, for by attracting the elect to himself through faith and love, he takes them up into himself, just as the cheeks take up items of food. As the Savior says in John 4 [32]: "I have food to eat, which you know not." Literally this refers to the Samaritans, whom Christ took up into himself by faith. *As beds of aromatical spices,* because, just as a pleasant odor rises from a bed of sweet-smelling spices, refreshing to the sense of smell, so God's love, which has power to draw things to itself, renews the souls of the righteous. *His lips* are the power which God has to reserve secrets for those he calls saints and prophets. The text therefore adds, *as lilies dropping choice myrrh,* because the words of the Lord are pure and preserved from the corruption of sin.

[Ch. 5:14] *His hands* are God's power to control, *turned and as of gold,* or, according to the Hebrews, *of a gold wheel,* for by a wheel's circular shape the perfection of God's divine works is referred to, as in Deuteronomy 32 [4]: "The works of God are perfect." *His stomach* refers to God's unsearchable judgments, the same way that it is often said about a man in hiding, "you cannot tell what he has in his stomach." *Ivory,* for ivory is cold and white, and pondering God's unsearchable judgments causes people to refrain from sin out of cold fear, as it says in Proverbs 15 [27]: "By the fear of the Lord everyone declineth from evil." Thus the soul is purified and adorned with the desire for heavenly life. The text therefore adds, *set with sapphires,* since heaven is the color of sapphires.

[Ch. 5:15] *His legs* are the power by which God sustains all things, *[set upon] bases of gold,* placed under the divine or of the person. *His form as of Libanus, excellent as the cedars,* since God's beauty is most pleasing, and his stature is incomprehensible.

[Ch. 5:16] *His throat most sweet, and he is all lovely,* because God is infinitely good. *Such is my beloved* etc., as if to say, I believe with my heart and confess with my mouth that I ought to love him above all things.

[Ch. 5:17] *Whither is [thy beloved] gone?* This question arises from what precedes it. In truth, those who do penance and make confession are aided on their journey to God by his saints. Therefore, in the person of the saints the text asks, *Whither is thy beloved gone?,* as if to say, "We are ready to help you to be reconciled to God." And the text adds, *We will seek [him with thee].* However, that question,

pus captionis archae per Philisteos et translationis eius ad terram illorum. Tunc enim dicitur Deus abiisse de terra Israel eo quod propitiatorium super archam existens locus Dei dicebatur. *O pulcherrima mulierum,* id est, omnium gentium tempore desponsationis tuae cum Deo per legis susceptionem. *Quo abiit,* repetitio est eiusdem ad maiorem expressionem. *Quo declinavit.* Hoc refertur ad tempus reductionis archae in Bethsames, non opere humano, sed divino, I Reg. VI. *Et quaeremus eum tecum.* Hoc refertur ad tempus in quo David devotus ivit cum sacerdotibus et Levitis ad reducendum solemniter et devote archam Domini in Hierusalem, II Reg. VI ca.

Cap. VI.

Dilectus meus. Hic consequenter describitur amor sponsi et sponsae pro tempore David usque ad Christum. Ed dividitur in quatuor partes quia primo tangitur tempus ipsius David, secundo Salomonis, ibi: *Descendi in hortum,* tertio tempus regum sequentium usque ad captivitatem Babylonicam, ibi: *Nescivi,* quarto tempus post captivitatem praedictam, ibi: *Revertere.* Prima in duas, quia primo ponitur sponsae reconciliatae gratiarum actio, secundo eiusdem commendatio, ibi: *Pulchra es.* Circa primum sciendum quod reducta archa in Hierusalem per David ut praedictum est qui instituit sacerdotes et Levitas ad laudandum Deum, I Parali. XVI, apparuit benignitas Dei et eius reconciliatio erga populum Israel, propter quod regratians sponsa dicit: *Dilectus meus descendit in hortum suum,* id est, intra tabernaculum quod tetendit David ad collationem archae, II Reg. VI. *Ut ibi pascatur in hortis,* id est, delectetur in sacrificiis et oblationibus ex fide et devotione oblatis, sicut de sacrificio Noe dicitur, Gen. VIII: Odoratusque est Dominus odorem suavitatis. *Et lilia colligat,* id est, ministros mundos ad suum ministerium applicet.

Ego dilecto meo, id est, ipsi soli servire volo. *Et dilectus meus mihi,* necessitatibus meis subveniendo.

Whither is [thy beloved] gone?, could also refer to the time when the ark was captured by the Philistines and carried off to their land. Then God was said to have departed from the land of Israel, since the mercy seat, situated above the ark, was called the place where God dwelt. *O thou most beautiful among women,* that is, in comparison with all other nations, when you were espoused by God through receiving his Law. *Whither is [thy beloved] gone?* The question is repeated in order to make a greater impression. *Whither is [thy beloved] turned aside?* This refers to the time when the ark was returned at Bethsames, not by human endeavor but by divine, 1 Kings 6. *We will seek him with thee.* This refers to the time when holy David journeyed with the priests and Levites to return the ark of the Lord solemnly and devoutly to Jerusalem, 2 Kings 6.

[Ch. 6:1] *My beloved [is gone down].* Next we have the description of the love between the groom and bride from David's time to Christ's. It is divided into four parts. First the time of David himself is mentioned. Second, the time of Solomon, beginning at the words, *I went down into the garden* [ch. 6:10]. Third, the time of the kings who followed Solomon until the Babylonian Captivity is treated, beginning at the words, *I know not* [ch.6:12]. Fourth, the time after the captivity is covered, beginning at the word *Return* [ch. 6:12]. The first of these four parts is subdivided into two parts. First comes the thanks which the reconciled bride offered. Second, there is praise for the bride at the words, *Thou art beautiful* [ch. 6:3]. Pertaining to the thanks which the bride offered, one must bear in mind that when the ark was returned to Jerusalem by David, as just mentioned, he instructed the priests and Levites to praise God, 1 Paralipomenon [1 Chronicles] 16 [7]. God's goodness toward the Israelites and his reconciliation with them were clearly apparent. Therefore the bride, thankful for this, says, *My beloved is gone down into his garden,* that is, into the tabernacle which David built to house the ark, 2 Kings 6 [17], *to feed in the gardens,* that is, in order to take pleasure in the sacrifices and offerings which were made out of faith, and the things which were offered out of devotion, as it says about Noah's sacrifice in Genesis 8 [21]: "And the Lord smelled a sweet savor," *and to gather lilies,* that is, in order to appoint ministers, who were ceremonially clean, to serve him.

[Ch. 6:2] *I to my beloved,* that is, I want to serve this one and no other, *and my beloved to me,* that is, I want him to aid me in all my needs.

Pulchra es. Hic consequenter sponsus sponsam commendat ex gratitudine dicta, dicens: *Pulchra es amica mea,* id est, ad pulchritudinem pristinam restituta. *Suavis,* ex devotione mentis. *Et decora,* ex honestate conversationis. *Sicut Hierusalem,* quae fuit electa specialiter in locum divini cultus, et similiter populus Israel electus fuit ad colendum Deum prae ceteris gentibus. *Terribilis ut castrorum acies ordinata,* quia tempore David in populo Israel et in Hierusalem viguit militia.

Averte oculos tuos a me etc., intelligitur per oppositum, et est modus loquendi amantium ad expressionem amoris mutui, sicut sponsus dicit aliquando sponsae praedilectae: Vade non curo de te, per hoc gestum insinuans quod diligit eam intime, sicut aliquando de puero albo et gratioso dicitur: Ecce puer maurulus, insinuando per oppositum eius pulchritudinem. Aliter etiam exponitur de studiosis in lege qui aliquando inquirunt divina nimis curiose, et sic Deus retrahit se ab eis, et sic dicitur ab eis avolare. Per hoc ergo quod dicitur: *Averte* etc., inhibetur divinorum inquisitio curiosa, Prov. XXV: Qui perscrutator est maiestatis opprimetur a gloria. *Capilli tui* etc., exponatur ut supra IIII ca. usque ibi:

Sexaginta sunt reginae etc., per hoc ut dicit Rabbi Salomon intelliguntur LX personae descendentes ab Abraham, scilicet, Isaac et duo filii eius, Ismael et XII filii eius, et filii de Cethura XVI, et filii Iacob XII, et filii Esau XVI. *Et octoginta concubinae,* id est, LXXX personae de Noe usque ad Abraham exclusive, et istae numerationes accipiuntur ex I Parali. ca. I. Et sicut reginae sunt maiores concubinis regum, ita personae descendentes ab Abraham praedictae propter magnitudinem fidei Abrahe exprimuntur nobiliori nomine quam descendentes a Noe. *Et adolescentularum,* id est, cognationum et gentium a praedictis descendentium. *Non est numerus,* id est, sunt valde multae.

Una est columba mea, id est, de omnibus praedictis gentibus non elegi nisi unam in sponsam, scilicet, populum Israel, quem desponsavi per legem. Aliter etiam potest exponi, quod licet solum in Hierusalem fieret oblatio sacrificiorum, tamen in singulis

[Ch. 6:3] *Thou art beautiful.* Next the groom praises the bride out of gratitude for what she has said, saying, *Thou art beautiful, O my love,* that is, you are restored to pristine beauty, *sweet,* from your devotion to me with your mind, *and comely,* from the purity of your association with me, *as Jerusalem,* which was chosen in a special way to be the place for divine worship. Similarly, the Israelites were chosen above all other nations to worship God. *Terrible as an army set in array,* because in David's time the army flourished among the Israelites and in Jerusalem.

[Ch. 6:4] *Turn away thy eyes from me,* etc., is to be understood in the opposite way. This is the way lovers speak in order to express their love for each other. For example, a groom sometimes says to his beloved bride, "Go away, I don't care about you." By this expression he actually means he loves her intensely. Or, sometimes people say about a handsome, fair-skinned boy, "Look at the black boy," meaning instead his beauty. In still another way, this concept is applied to students of the Law who sometimes inquire into divine matters with a little too much curiosity, so that God withdraws from them. God is then said to fly away from them. Therefore, this phrase *Turn away,* etc., prohibits searching into divine matters with too much curiosity, as it says in Proverbs 25 [27]: "He that is a searcher of majesty, shall be overwhelmed by glory." *Thy hair,* etc., should be understood the same way as above in chapter four [ch. 4:2].

[Ch. 6:7] *There are threescore queens.* By this, says Rabbi Solomon, the sixty persons descended from Abraham are meant, namely, Isaac and his two sons, Ishmael and his twelve sons, the sixteen sons of Cetura, the twelve sons of Jacob, and the sixteen sons of Esau. *And fourscore concubines,* that is, the eighty persons from Noah to Abraham. These numbers are taken from 1 Paralipomenon, chapter one. And just as queens are greater than kings' concubines, so those who are descendants of Abraham are considered to be nobler than those who are descendants of Noah, due to the greatness of Abraham's faith. *And young maidens,* that is, the relatives and nations which are descended from those people just mentioned, *without number,* that is, there are very many of them.

[Ch. 6:8] *One is my dove,* that is, of all the above-mentioned nations, only one was chosen as the bride, namely, the Israelites, whom God espoused to himself by giving them the Law. This phrase can also be explained in a different way: Though the offering of sacrifices

civitatibus, oppidis, et villulis Iudaeae erant loca ubi congregabatur populus ad orationem et ad audiendum legem divinam, et dicebantur synagogae, igitur per reginas possunt intelligi synagogae civitatum, per concubinas oppidorum, et forte iste et ille erant in tali numero, vel ponitur hic numerus determinatus per indeterminato, sicut alibi in Scriptura, Dan. VII: Decies milies centena milia assistebant ei. Angeli enim assistentes Deo sunt in multo maiori numero secundum omnes expositores. Per unam quae dicitur columba et sponsa, intelligitur tabernaculum ubi in Hierusalem erat archa, quia prae ceteris civitatibus et locis erat ad Dei cultum electa, et dicitur: *Electa matris suae,* id est, Ecclesiae triumphanti quae dicitur mater militantis, Gal. IIII. Illa quae sursum est Hierusalem libera est, quae est mater nostra. *Viderunt eam filiae Syon,* etc., id est, populus de civitate Hierusalem et aliis civitatibus et locis Iudaeae commendaverunt cultum Dei qui erat in Hierusalem, propter quod admirative de profectu Ecclesiae tempore David subditur:

Quae est ista quae progreditur quasi aurora consurgens. Inter illa quae apparent de die sol habet maiorem pulchritudinem et luna de nocte, et aurora inter diem et noctem, et per hoc intelligitur pulchritudo Ecclesiae tempore David qui cultum divinum valde augumentavit, I Parali. XXIII usque ad XXVII, ita quod non fuerat ante pulchrior tempore prosperitatis quod significatur per diem, nec adversitatis quod per noctem, nec status intermedii quod per auroram.

Descendi. Hic consequenter describitur amor sponsi et sponsae pro tempore Salomonis qui aedificavit Domino templum nobilissimum, et in eius dedicatione descendit divinitas in signo visibili nebulae, III Reg. VIII, propter quod tunc ait Salomon: Dominus dixit ut habitaret in nebula propter hoc ergo dicit sponsus hic: *Descendi in hortum nucum,* id est, in Salomonis templum, quod erat quasi Dei umbraculum. *Ut viderem poma convallium,* id est, opera bona humilium. *Et inspicerem si floruisset vinea,* id est, Israel Ecclesia, Isa. V:

took place only in Jerusalem, there were also places called synagogues in the individual cities, towns, and villages of Judea, where people gathered to pray and to hear God's Law. Therefore, "queens" can be interpreted as the synagogues in the cities, and "concubines" as the synagogues in the towns. Perhaps the former numbered sixty, and the latter eighty, or perhaps here a definite number is used for an indefinite number, as happens elsewhere in Scripture. For example, in Daniel 7 [10] we read: "Ten thousand times a hundred thousand stood before him." The angels standing before God were actually much greater in number, according to all interpreters. The one who is called a "dove" and a "bride," means the tabernacle where the ark was housed in Jerusalem. Because Jerusalem was chosen over all other cities and places for worshiping God, the text says, *Chosen of her mother,* that is, the Church triumphant, which is called the mother of the Church militant, as it says in Galatians 4 [26]: "But that Jerusalem which is above is free, which is our mother." *The daughters of Sion saw her* etc., that is, the people of the city of Jerusalem and of other cities and places in Judea praised the worship of God which was carried on in Jerusalem. Because of the wonderful success of the Church during the time of David, the text adds:

[Ch. 6:9] *Who is she that cometh forth as the morning rising?* Among things which we can see, the sun has greater beauty by day and the moon by night, with dawn between them. This should be applied to the beauty of the Church during the time of David who greatly advanced the worship of God, as 1 Paralipomenon 23-27 shows. He did so to such an extent that the Church was never more beautiful, either before this wonderful time, which is signified by "day," nor in any time of adversity, signified by "night," nor at any time between them, signified by "dawn."

[Ch. 6:10] *I went down.* Next we have the mutual love of the groom and bride during the time of Solomon, who built a most splendid temple for the Lord. At its dedication, God descended visibly in the form of a cloud, 3 Kings 8 [12]. When this happened, Solomon said, "The Lord said that he would dwell in a cloud." In view of this event, then, the groom says, *I went down into the garden of nuts,* that is, God descended into the temple of Solomon, where he dwelt in the shadows, *to see the fruits of the valleys,* that is, the good works of his humble people, *and to look if the vineyard had flourished,* that is, if the Israelite Church had flourished, as it says in Isaiah 5 [7]: "For the

Vinea enim Domini exercituum domus Israel est, quae floruit tempore David et Salomonis. *Et germinassent mala punica,* id est, sacerdotes et Levitae eo quod malogranata posita erant in margine tunicae summi sacerdotis qui erat caput aliorum, propter quod in eo virtualiter intelliguntur alii ministri propter similitudinem tunicae in qua erant depicta mala punica, Exo. XXVIII, tempore vero Salomonis germinavit summi sacerdotis officium, quia abiecto Abiathar factus est Sadoch summus sacerdos, III Reg. II, et sic fuit restitutum summum sacerdotium filiis Eleazari filii Aaron quod usurpaverat Heli qui descenderat de Ithamar.

Nescivi. Hic consequenter ponitur status sponsae post tempus Salomonis usque ad captiviatem Babylonis, breviter tamen et succincte. Circa quod sciendum quod mortuo Salomone statim populus Israeli quantum ad decem tribus declinavit ad idolatriam per deceptionem Hieroboam, III Reg. XII, et postea aliae duae tribus similiter coluerunt idola, maxime tempore Achaz et Menasse regum Iuda, ut patet IIII Reg., propter quod decem tribus primo fuerunt captivatae per regem Assyriorum, IIII Reg. XVIII, et postea aliae duae per regem Babylonis, IIII Reg. XXV, propter quod lamentando dicit sponsa: *Nescivi,* considerare circa me beneficia Dei temporibus praeteritis exhibita. *Anima mea conturbavit me,* timore ad idolatriam inducente. Hieroboam enim timore perdendi regnum decem tribuum induxit populum ad idolatriam, ne si iret in Hierusalem ad colendum Dominum reverteretur ad priorem dominum, scilicet, ad Roboam filium Salomonis, ideo subditur: *Propter quadrigas Aminadab,* per quas intelligitur potentia regni Iudae, eo quod tribus Iuda secundum omnes doctores Hebraicos et Latinos meruit dignitatem regiam in transitu Maris Rubri. Nam aliis tribubus formidantibus Moysen sequi per mare divisum, tribus Iuda constantur secuta fuit ipsum et aliis constantiae dedit exemplum, tunc autem Aminadab erat princeps tribus Iudae qui egressus est de Aegypto cum Naason filio suo, qui mortuo patre successit ei in principatu, Numeri VII. Hebraei dicunt quod haec est vera littera: *Anima mea posuit me quadrigas populi*

vineyard of the Lord of hosts is the house of Israel." In fact, this vineyard did flourish during the time of David and Solomon. *And [if] the pomegranates budded,* that is, the priests and Levites in the sense that pomegranates were embroidered on the hem of the high priest's tunic, the priest who was superior to all other priests. Actually, since all priests wore similarly decorated tunics, all priests are included here, as we learn from Exodus 28 [33-34]. As a matter of fact, the office of the high priest "budded" in the time of Solomon, because after Abiathar was rejected, Sadoch was made the high priest, 3 Kings 2 [27-35], and thus the high priesthood was restored to the sons of Eleazar, the son of Aaron, the office which Eli, who descended from Ithamar, had usurped.

[Ch. 6:11] *I knew not.* Next comes the bride's situation from Solomon's time up to the Babylonian Captivity, but it is only touched on briefly with a few words. At this point you have to keep in mind that, after the death of Solomon, ten tribes of the Israelites immediately turned to idolatry, misled by Jeroboam, 3 Kings 12. Later, the other two tribes also worshiped idols, especially during the time when Ahaz and Manassas were kings of Judea, as is clear from 4 Kings. Because of this, first the ten tribes were taken captive by the king of Assyria, 4 Kings 18, and later the other two tribes were taken captive by the king of Babylon, 4 Kings 25. Because of these events the bride laments, *I knew not* how to regard the blessings of God shown to me in past times. *My soul troubled me,* with my fear leading me into idolatry. For Jereboam was afraid that if the Israelites went to worship God in Jerusalem, they would again give their allegiance to their rightful Lord, Rehoboam, the son of Solomon. So he enticed the people into idolatry, and thereby destroyed the kingdom of the ten tribes. *For the chariots of Aminadab.* This should be understood as a reference to the prominence of the kingdom of Judea, for the tribe of Judah, according to all Hebrew and Latin doctors, merited the honor of being the royal tribe by the way it crossed the Red Sea. For when the other tribes were afraid to follow Moses through the sea after it had parted, the tribe of Judah followed him and thereby set an example of steadfastness for the other tribes. At that time, Aminadab was the leader of the tribe of Judah. He had left Egypt with Nahasson his son, who, after the death of his father, succeeded him as the leader, Numbers 7. The Hebrew interpreters say that the text should actually be translated as, *My soul set me for the chariots of the ruling people.*

principantis, ita quod Aminadab non est hic unum nomen proprium, sed sunt duo nomina significantia populum principantem, et sic est sensus: *Anima mea,* id est, voluntas mea quae sic nominatur frequenter in Scriptura, eo quod movet alias animae potentias ad agendum, voluntas vero perversa induxit populum ad idolatrandum, propter quod fuit captivatus ut dictum est, ideo sequitur: *Posuit me quadrigas populi principantis,* scilicet, Assyriorum et Babyloniorum qui ducebant filios Israeli captivitatem sicut quadrigas oneratas, imponentes eis onera gravia in itinere ad portandum.

Revertere. Hic consequenter tangitur status populi a reditu captivitatis Babylonicae usque ad Christum, breviter tamen et succincte, et secundum hoc dicitur: *Revertere, revertere,* scilicet, de captivitate. *Sunamitis.* Sic nominatur hic sponsa a civitate nomine Suna in qua pluries hospitatus fuit Heliseus, ut habetur IIII Reg. IIII. In Hebraeo sic habetur: *Revertere, revertere, Sulamit,* et si trabatur ad proprietatem Latinam dicitur *Sulamitis,* id est, integra vel perfecta, quasi diceret, revertere ad statum pristinum perfectionis tuae, vel melius ad statum integrum fidei tuae, quia post reditum captivitatis Babylonicae semper fuit populus Israel in subiectione, primo Persarum, secundo Graecorum, tertio Romanorum, stetit tamen fideliter in cultu unius Dei veri usque ad Christum. Et dicitur hic quater *revertere,* quia primo aliqui redierunt de Babylone cum Zorobabel duce, secundo aliqui cum Esdra sacerdote, I Esdrae VII, tertio aliqui cum Neemia, quarto tempore Iude Machabei qui propter persecutionem Antiochi fugerat ad loca deserta, et postea rediit ad civitates et loca sua habita victoria de ducibus Antiochi, ut habetur I Machab. *Ut intueamur te,* colentem Deum in terra Iuda. Verumtamen quia temporibus illis populus Israel molestatus fuit ab aliis populis, propter quod oportebat eum frequenter pugnare, propter quod subditur:

Quid videbis in Sunamite vel *Sulamite,* secundum litteram Hebraicam. *Nisi choros castrorum,* id est, societates ad pugnam paratorum, quia tempore Neemiae in reparatione civitatis una manu faciebant opus, et altera tenebant gladium, et media pars populi erat

Aminadab, then, is not a proper noun in the singular, but really two nouns which mean "ruling people." The sense would then be: *My soul,* that is, my will, which is often called "soul" in Scripture, since it moves a person to action. In fact, it was a wicked will which led the people into idolatry, which is why they were taken captive, as I already explained. What you have then is this: *[My soul] set me for the chariots of the ruling people,* meaning that the Assyrians and Babylonians led the children of Israel into captivity as if they were loaded chariots, setting heavy loads on them to carry on their journey.

[Ch. 6:12] *Return.* Next the situation of the Israelites after their return from the Babylonian Captivity up to Christ is touched on briefly and also succinctly. About this the text says, *Return, return,* that is, from captivity, *O Sunamitis.* The bride is here given a name derived from the city of Suna, where Elisha received much hospitality, as we learn from 4 Kings 4 [8]. The Hebrew text actually says, *Return, return, Sulamit,* and if this were translated into correct Latin, it would be *Sulamitis,* meaning "complete" or "perfect." The meaning would then be, "Return to the time when you were a perfect nation," or better, "Return to the time when your faith was perfect," since after the Israelites returned from the Babylonian Captivity they were always under subjection to someone, first to the Persians, then the Greeks, and finally the Romans, though the Israelites did remain faithful in their worship of the one true God up to the time of Christ. The word *Return* is repeated four times, because, first of all, some returned from Babylon under the leadership of Zorobabel. Later some returned under Esdras the priest, 1 Esdras 7. Still later, some returned under Nehemiah. And finally, some returned during the time of Judas Maccabeus, who, because of the persecution of Antiochus, had fled to a place in the desert. Later, after he was victorious over Antiochus's generals, he returned to the cities of his region, as described in 1 Maccabees. *That we may behold thee,* that is, in order to worship God in the land of Judah. But since the Israelites upon their return were continually harassed by other nations, so that they had to protect themselves, the text goes on:

[Ch. 7:1a] *What shalt thou see in the Sunamitis* (or *the Sulamitis* in the Hebrew text) *but the companies of camps?,* that is, groups of men preparing to fight. For at the time of Nehemiah, while rebuilding the city of Jerusalem, the men had to work with one hand, and in the other hand they held a sword, and the main body of the Israelites

armata ad melius resistendum adversariis, Neemiae IIII, et postea
Machabeorum tempore populus Israel fuit in bellis quasi continue
ut patet ex decursu I et II Machabaeorum.

Cap. VII.

Quam pulchri sunt. Postquam descriptus est amor sponsi et
sponsae pro statu Veteris Testamenti, hic consequenter idem
describitur pro statu Novi, et dividitur in tres partes, quia primo
ponitur huius status inchoatio, secundo inchoati dilatatio, ibi: *Veni
dilecte mi,* tertio dilatati tranquillatio, sequente ca. Circa primum
describitur sponsa primo generaliter, secundo quantum ad perfectos
specialiter, ibi: *Dixi ascendam.* Circa primum describitur sponsa sub
parabola mulieris gratiosae, alter tamen quam supra IIII ca., quia ibi
describit sponsae pulchritudinem a superioribus incipiendo, et ad
inferiora descendendo, hic autem econverso incipiendo ab inferioribus
ad superiora tendendo, quia pro tempore Veteris Testamenti sponsa
quasi a Deo procedit et egreditur pro tempore vero Novi de terrenis
ad caelestia in Deum reducitur. Igitur primo parabola pulchrae
mulieris ponetur, secundo exponetur. Quantum ad primum sic
dicitur: *Quam pulchri sunt,* id est, valde pulchri. *Gressus tui in
calciamentis,* ad gratiositatem enim mulieris multum facit quod mature et honeste incedit et calciatis pedibus, quia inhonestum est quod
nuda pedibus appareat. *Iuncturae femorum tuorum sicut monilia quae
fabricata sunt manu artificis,* per hoc designatur quod crura sunt in
iuncturis suis debite collocata ad excludendam omnimodam
claudicationem.

Umbilicus tuus sicut crater tornatilis, id est, rotundus et
beneformatus, et accipitur hic *umbilicus* pro superficie ventris in cuius
medio est umbilicus. In Hebraeo habetur: *Umbilicus tuus bacinus
clarus,* in quo designatur pulchra dispositio ventris exterius. *Venter
tuus sicut acervus tritici,* id est, interius fecundus in prole. *Vallatus
liliis,* id est, decoratus maritali castitate.

Duo ubera tua sicut duo hinnuli gemelli capreae, id est, equaliter
tumentia et abundantia lacte pro prole nutrienda.

Collum tuum sicut turris eburnea, id est, rectum ad modum turris,
et album ad modum eboris. *Oculi tui sicut piscinae in Esebon.* Secundum Hebraeos Esebon non est hic nomen civitatis ultra Iordanem

was armed in order to successfully resist their enemies, Nehemiah 4. Later, during Maccabean times, the Israelites engaged in wars almost continually, as is shown clearly in 1 and 2 Maccabees.

[Ch. 7:1b] *How beautiful are [thy steps]*. Now that the love between the groom and bride has been described during Old Testament times, it will be described during the New Testament. This is divided into three parts. First we have the situation at the beginning of this time period. Then we have what follows, beginning at the words, *Come, my beloved* [ch. 7:11]. Finally, we have the peacefulness at the end of this period, in the next chapter. Pertaining to the first of these three parts we have the bride described first in a general way, then more specifically, beginning at the words, *I said, I will go up* [ch. 7:8]. In the first of these sub-parts the bride is described by using the parable of a good-looking wife, but differently from above in chapter four. There the bride's beauty was described from her head down. Here, conversely, it is described from her feet up. For during the Old Testament the bride went away from God and passed out of his presence. However, during the New Testament, she was led back to God, her direction turned from earthly affairs to heavenly. First, then, comes the parable of the beautiful wife, then the explanation. Pertaining to her beauty the text says: *How beautiful are thy steps,* that is, they are very beautiful, *in shoes,* since the quality of a woman is greatly enhanced if she walks in a mature and proper manner with her feet nicely shod, and, conversely, it is improper for her to go barefoot. *The joints of thy thighs are like jewels, that are made by the hand of a skillful workman.* This means that her legs are not out of joint, which would cause her to walk with a limp.

[Ch. 7:2] *Thy navel is like a round bowl,* that is, it is round and well formed. *Navel* here stands for the whole stomach, in the middle of which is the navel. The Hebrew text has: *Thy navel is a clear basin,* which refers to the beautiful, outward appearance of the stomach. *Thy stomach is like a heap of wheat,* that is, on the inside it is fruitful in bearing children, *set about with lilies,* that is, adorned with marital chastity.

[Ch. 7:3] *Thy two breasts are like two young roes that are twins,* that is, both are filled with abundant milk for nursing children.

[Ch. 7:4] *Thy neck as a tower of ivory,* that is, erect like a tower, and white like ivory. *Thy eyes like the fishpools in Hesebon.* According to the Hebrew interpreters, "Hesebon" here is not the name of the

de qua dicitur Numeri XXII [XXI]: Ignis egressus est de Esebon, sed
est nomen commune significas computationem. Et sic est litteram:
Oculi tui sicut piscinae in computationem, id est, magnae reputationis.
Quae sunt in porta, id est, prope portam. *Filiae multitudinis,* id est,
Hierusalem, quae dicitur multitudinis filia, eo quod erat plena populo,
Trenn. I, erant enim duae piscinae aquarum in Hierusalam, civitatem
multum decorantes sicut oculi pulchri et mundi decorant mulierem.
Comparantur autem oculi piscinis aquarum, eo quod sunt aquaei a
dominio [*sic*], propter quod si laedantur, in lachrymis resolvuntur.
Nasus tuus sicut turris Libani, id est, rectus et bene sedens in facie
sicut turris Libani quae erat recta et bene sita in extremitate terrae
promissionis. *Contra Damascum,* quae erat civitas Syriorum qui frequenter fuerant adversarii Iudaeorum.

Caput tuum ut Carmelus, supereminens corpori, et bene sedens
sicut Mons Carmelus in terra promissionis qui est frugifer et gratiosus,
Isaie XXXV: Gloria Libani data est ei, decor Carmeli et Saron. *Et
comae ... iuncta canalibus,* id est, posita in canalibus ad lavandum
post tincturam ut color sit magis vividus, per hoc designatur
pulchritudo capillorum sponsae in colore *sicut purpura* quae tingitur
pro paramentis regiis sit coloris excellentis, ideo subditur:

Quam pulchra es etc.

Statura tua assimilata est palmae, id est, recta est et alta *Et ubera
tua botris,* propter ubertatem lactis. Omnia praedicta faciunt ad
gratiositatem sponsae corporalis. Per dictam parabolam intelligitur
ad litteram decor sponsae spiritualis pro tempore Novi Testamenti,
de qua dicitur:

Quam pulchri sunt gressus tui, per evangelica consilia gradiendo.
In calciamentis, calciamenta quae fiunt de pellibus animalium
mortuorum sunt memoria mortis Christi et martyrum quae muniunt
pedes sponsae ad firmiter incedendum per consilia evangelii. *Filia principis,*

city across the Jordan River, about which Numbers 22 [Numbers 21:28] says, "A fire is gone out of Hesebon." Rather here they say "Hesebon" is a common noun meaning "comparison." So literally we have: *Thy eyes are like the fishpools in comparison,* that is, they are widely admired, *which are in the gate,* that is, the fishpools are next to the gate, *of the daughter of the multitude,* that is, the gate of Jerusalem, which is called the daughter of the multitude in the sense that it was full of people, Threni [Lamentations] 1:1. Bear in mind that there were two fishpools in Jerusalem, each of which added greatly to the city's beauty, just as clear, beautiful eyes add a great deal to a woman's beauty. Besides this, her eyes are compared to watery fishpools in the sense that they are waters of the master, on account of which if they are injured they are healed with tears. *Thy nose is as the tower of Libanus,* that is, straight and nicely positioned on the face, just as the tower of Lebanon stood erect and well positioned at the border of the Promised Land. *[That looketh] toward Damascus,* which was a city of the Syrians who frequently were enemies of the Jews.

[Ch. 7:5] *Thy head is like Carmel.* The head is the high point of the body, and well placed, just as Mt. Carmel in the Promised Land, which was a delightful and fruitful place. As it says in Isaiah 35 [2]: "The glory of Lebanon is given to it, the beauty of Carmel and Saron." *And the hairs [of thy head as the purple of the king] bound in the channels,* that is, put into channels for washing after it has been dyed, so that the color might be more vivid. This signifies the beautiful color of the bride's hair, just as the beautiful purple-dyed color of a king's robe signifies his royalty. Therefore the text adds:

[Ch. 7:6] *How beautiful art thou, [and how comely, my dearest, in delights].*

[Ch. 7:7] *Thy stature is like to a palm tree,* that is, straight and tall, *and thy breasts to clusters of grapes,* because they are filled with milk. Everything said so far indicates the beauty of the human bride. But literally this parable signifies the beauty of the spiritual bride during the time of the New Testament. About this the text says:

[Ch. 7:1b] *How beautiful are thy steps,* by walking in accordance with the evangelical counsels. *In shoes.* Shoes, which are made from the hides of dead animals, are a reminder of the death of Christ and the martyrs. [As shoes protect the human bride's feet, so] the death of Christ and the martyrs enable the spiritual bride to walk firmly in line with the evangelical counsels. *O prince's daughter,* that is, the

id est, Ecclesia quae dicitur filia et sponsa Christi qui est princeps regum terrae, Apoc. I. *Iuncturae femorum tuorum,* id est, coniunctio Iudaeorum et Gentilium in una Christi Ecclesia. Et haec iunctura *fabricata est manu artificis,* id est, Christi qui fecit utraque unum, Eph. II.

Umbilicus tuus etc. Per umbilicum sub quo fetus concipitur, et per ventrem in quo ante nativitatem alitur, intelligitur Ecclesiae fecunditas ad gignendum filios ipsi Christo, et quia non generantur carnaliter, sed spiritualiter, Joh. I: Qui non ex sanguinibus neque ex voluntate carnis etc. Ideo venter ille dicitur: *Vallatus liliis,* scilicet, castitatis.

Duo ubera tua, id est, duo Testamenta ex quibus suggitur lac quo nutriuntur et augmentantur filii in Christo generati, I Petri II: Quasi modo geniti infantes rationabiles sine dolo lac concupiscite ut in eo crescatis in salutem.

Collum tuum, id est, fides formata caritate quae coniungit corpus sponsae capiti suo Christo, Eph. I: Ipsum dedit caput super omnem Ecclesiam. Huius autem capitis *nasus* est iudicium discretionis quo in praesenti discernit fideles ab infidelibus, sicut nasus discernit inter odores fetidos et suaves. *Oculi* vero sunt Christi virtus cognitiva quibus respicit fideles suos eos approbando, Ioh. X: Ego cognosco oves meas, qui dicuntur fideles. *Sicut piscinae,* quia pleni sunt aquis misericordiae.

Caput tuum, id est, huius capitis summitas quae est Christi divinitas, ex quo capite fluit sensus et motus vitae spiritualis, primo in humanitatem Christi, et consequenter ad omnia membra Ecclesiae. Ideo subditur: *Sicut Carmelus,* qui est mons fructibus plenus. *Comae huius capitis* sunt apostoli qui primo adhaeserunt Christo capiti, qui dicuntur: *Sicut purpura regis,* quia pro amore regis Christi fuerunt suo sanguine rubricati per palmam martyrii. Ex praedictis concluditur:

Church, which is called the daughter and the bride of Christ, who is the head of the kings of the world, Apocalypse 1 [5]. *The joints of thy thighs,* that is, the union of Jews and Gentiles in one Church of Christ. And this union is *made by the hand of a skillful workman,* that is, it comes about through Christ, who made both one, Ephesians 2 [10].

[Ch. 7:2] *Thy navel [is like a round bowl never wanting cups. Thy stomach is like a heap of wheat].* The navel, under which the fetus is conceived, and the stomach, in which it is nourished before birth, signify the fruitfulness of the Church in producing sons for Christ. And because such sons are not born according to the flesh but according to the spirit—as it says in John 1 [13]: "Who [are born], not of blood, nor of the will of the flesh," [nor of the will of man, but of God]—therefore the stomach is described as *set about with lilies,* that is, chastity.

[Ch. 7:3] *Thy two breasts,* that is, the two Testaments, from which the milk is sucked which nourishes the sons born for Christ and causes them to grow, as it says in 1 Peter 2 [2]: "As newborn babes, desire the rational milk without guile, that thereby you may grow unto salvation."

[Ch. 7:4] *Thy neck,* that is, faith formed by love, which unites the bride's body to Christ, her head, as Ephesians 1 [22] says: "He hath made him head over all the Church." Besides this, *the nose* on his face is his power to judge with discretion, by which he distinguishes the faithful from the unfaithful in this present age, just as a nose distinguishes between good and bad odors. Also, *the eyes* are the cognitive power of Christ by which he looks over his faithful people with approval, as it says in John 10 [14]: "I know my sheep," which refers to his faithful people, *like the fishpools,* because his eyes are filled with the waters of loving-kindness.

[Ch. 7:5] *Thy head,* that is, the crown of Christ's head, namely, his divinity, from which flow the intellectual and emotional qualities of the spiritual life, first into Christ according to his human nature, and then into all the members of his Church. In view of this the text adds, *like Carmel,* which is a mountain abundant in fruits. *The hairs of his* [Christ's] *head* are the first apostles to follow Christ as their head. They are said to be *as the purple of the king,* because out of love for Christ, their king, they were reddened with blood when they received the palm of martyrdom. Now comes the conclusion to what has been said:

Quam pulchra es, interius per fidem. *Et quam decora,* exterius per honestatem. *Carissima,* id est, precio maximo redempta, scilicet, sanguine Christi precioso. Illud enim carissimum dicitur quod maximo precio emitur. *In deliciis,* quia passio Christi aperuit portam deliciarum paradisi sponsae suae.

Statura tua assimilata est palmae, in rectitudine iusticiae et altitudine contemplationis devotae. *Et ubera tua botris,* propter abundantiam lactis ad nutritionem filiorum Christi et Ecclesiae.

Dixi ascendam. Hic consequenter describitur pulchritudo sponsae quantum ad perfectos specialiter, de quibus dicit sponsus: *Dixi ascendam,* id est, ascendere faciam perfectos in Ecclesia. *In palmam,* id est, in contemplationis altitudinem. *Et apprehendam,* id est, apprehendere faciam, sicut supra frequenter expositum est in simili. *Fructus eius,* id est, dulcedinem quae sentitur in contemplationis altitudine, sicut palma fructus suos facit in summitate. *Et erunt ubera tua sicut botri vineae,* ex abundantia lactis sacrae doctrinae. Contemplativi enim in contemplatione hauriunt quae postea per doctrinam effundunt, sicut patet de Paulo post eius raptum, et de multis aliis doctoribus. *Et odor oris tui,* id est, fama doctrinae. Unde Paulus Apostolus, II Cor. II: Per nos odorem suae noticiae manifestat in omni loco, quia Christi bonus odor sumus etc., et ad idem, pertinet quod subditur:

Guttur tuum, in quo formantur praedicationis verba. *Sicut vinum optimum,* inebrians amore divino mentes fidelium, et hoc est vinum germinans virgines, Zach IX. Et quia hoc est valde placidum Deo, ideo sequitur: *Dignum dilecto meo* etc., ideo concludit sponsa:

Ego dilecto meo, per amorem inhaereo. *Et ad me conversio eius,* consolando me in tribulationibus.

Veni dilecte. Hic consequenter describitur fidei Christi dilatatio quae primo fuit in Hierusalam, et inde derivata est ad alias partes orbis, sicut praedictum fuit Isa. II: De Syon exibit lex, et verbum Domini de Hierusalem, propter quod etiam dixit Christus apostolis Act. I: Eritis

[Ch. 7:6] *How beautiful art thou,* internally by virtue of faith, *and how comely,* externally by virtue of character, *[my] dearest,* that is, redeemed at the highest price, namely, by the precious blood of Christ. For whatever is bought at the highest price is called the dearest. *In delights,* because the passion of Christ opened the gate of the delights of paradise for his bride.

[Ch. 7:7] *Thy stature is like to a palm tree,* because Christ's justice is upright and his contemplation reaches the heights of holiness, *and thy breasts to clusters of grapes,* because Christ's breasts contain an abundance of milk for nursing his sons and the whole Church.

[Ch. 7:8] *I said I will go up.* Next the bride's beauty as it pertains specifically to the saints is described. The groom says, *I said, I will go up,* that is, I will cause saints to arise in the Church, *into the palm tree,* that is, into the heights of contemplation, *and I will take hold of,* that is, as I have already frequently explained in a similar way, I will cause the saints to take hold of *the fruit thereof,* that is, the sweetness which one senses when at the height of contemplation, just as the palm tree produces its fruit at the top. *And thy breasts shall be as the clusters of the vine,* because they contain an abundance of the milk of sacred doctrine. For while they are in contemplation, contemplatives absorb what they afterwards pour forth in their teaching, as can be clearly seen in the case of Paul after his vision, and in the lives of many other doctors of the Church. *And the odor of thy mouth,* that is, the renown of their teaching. As Paul the Apostle says in 2 Corinthians 2 [14-15]: "[Thanks be to God, who] manifesteth the odor of his knowledge by us in every place, for we are the good odor of Christ unto God." And what follows pertains to the same thing:

[Ch. 7:9] *Thy throat,* in which the words of prophecy take form, *like the best wine,* inebriating the minds of the faithful with divine love. This is the wine which produces virgins, as Zachariah 9 [15, 17] says. Because this is especially pleasing to God the text adds, *worthy for my beloved [to drink].* So the bride concludes:

[Ch. 7:10] *I to my beloved,* that is, I belong to him by loving him, *and his turning is towards me,* by the way he consoles me in my tribulations.

[Ch. 7:11] *Come [my] beloved.* Next the spread of faith in Christ is described. It began in Jerusalem, and from there it was dispersed to other parts of the world just as Isaiah prophesied in 2 [3]: "For the law shall come forth from Sion, and the word of the Lord from Jerusalem." Christ himself told his apostles in Acts 1 [8]: "You shall be

mihi testes in Hierusalem et in omni Iudaea atque Samaria et usque ad ultimum terrae, et hoc est quod petit sponsa hic: *Veni dilecte mi egrediamur in agrum,* per diffusionem fidei in orbe terrarum. *Commoremur in villis,* aedificando Ecclesias in civitatibus et villis.

Mane surgamus ad vineam, id est, ad convertendum Gentilitatem ex qua pro maiori parte est Ecclesia Christi quae dicitur eius vinea, sicut tempore Veteris Testamenti synagoga dicebatur Dei vinea, Isa. V: Vinea Domini exercituum domus Israel est, et dicitur: *Mane surgamus ad vineam,* quia in primitiva Ecclesia Iudaeis excecatis per infidelitatem, Gentilitas est illuminata per fidem, Ro. XI: Caecitas ex parte contigit in Israelis, donec plenitudo gentium intraret etc. *Videamus si floruerit vinea.* Hic accipitur si pro quia, quia Gentilitas floruit verbum Dei gaudenter accipiendo, Act. XIII: Audientes autem Gentes gavisae sunt et glorificabant verbum Domini. *Si flores fructus parturiunt,* si pro quia, quia Gentes non solum verbum Dei audierunt, sed etiam bonorum operum fructus fecerunt. *Si floruerunt mala punica,* per mala punica granis rubicundis plena, intelligitur plenitudo martyrorum in primitiva Ecclesia. *Ibi dabo tibi ubera mea,* id est, doctrinam utriusque Testamenti ad tuam gloriam ordinabo.

Mandragorae, poma sunt pulchra et odorifera et valde rara, et per hoc intelliguntur excellentes viri in Ecclesia Christi odorem famae per sanctam vitam et sanam doctrinam dantes in Ecclesia Dei, ideo subditur: *Omnia poma nova et vetera,* id est, Veteris ac Novi Testamenti testimonia. *Dilecte mi servavi tibi,* id est, ad honorem tuum ordinavi, propter quod dicit Salvator, Math. XIII: Omnis scriba doctus in regno caelorum similis est homini patrifamilias qui profert de thesauro suo nova et vetera.

Cap. VIII.

Quis mihi det. Hic ultimo describitur Ecclesiae Christi pacificatio. Et dividitur in duas partes, quia primo ponitur huius pacis desiderium, secundo complementum, ibi: *Soror nostra.* Prima adhuc in duas, quia

witnesses unto me in Jerusalem, and in all Judea, and Samaria, and even to the uttermost part of the earth." This is what the bride is asking for here, when she says, *Come, my beloved, let us go forth into the field,* by spreading the faith throughout the world. *Let us abide in the villages* by building churches in cities and villages.

[Ch. 7:12] *Let us get up early to the vineyard,* that is, to convert the Gentiles, who for the most part make up Christ's Church, which is called a vineyard, just as in Old Testament times the synagogue was called God's vineyard, in Isaiah 5 [7]: "For the vineyard of the Lord of hosts is the house of Israel." Furthermore, the text says, *Let us get up early to the vineyard,* because in the early Church, while the Jews remained blind by their unbelief, the Gentiles were enlightened by their faith, as Paul says in Romans 11 [25]: "Blindness in part has happened in Israel, until the fullness of the Gentiles should come in." *Let us see if the vineyard flourish.* Here "if" is used for "because," because [in fact] the Gentiles did flourish by accepting the word of God gladly, as Acts 13 [48] says: "And the Gentiles hearing it, were glad, and glorified the word of the Lord." *If the flowers be ready to bring forth fruits.* Again, "if" is used for "because," because the nations not only heard the word of God, but also produced the fruit of good works. *If the pomegranates flourish.* Pomegranates, which are full of red seeds, signify the great number of martyrs in the early Church. *There will I give thee my breasts,* that is, I will provide the teaching contained in both Testaments for your benefit.

[Ch. 7:13] *The mandrakes [give a smell].* Mandrakes are a beautiful, sweet-smelling, and very rare fruit, and this refers to the outstanding individuals in Christ's Church, who give off the sweet scent of their good reputation throughout God's Church by their holy life and pure teachings. The text then adds, *[In our gates are] all fruits; the new and the old,* that is, the testimony of the Old and New Testaments, *my beloved, I have kept for thee,* that is, I have provided these fruits for your benefit, as the Savior says in Matthew 13 [52]: "Every scribe instructed in the kingdom of heaven is like to a man that is a householder, who bringeth forth out of his treasure new things and old."

[Ch. 8:1] *Who shall give thee to me?* Finally, the peace which settled on Christ's Church is described. It is divided into two parts. First comes the desire for this peace. Then comes what complements this peace, beginning at the words, *Our sister* [ch. 8:8]. The first of these two parts is further divided into two sub-parts. First we have

primo desiderium hoc ponitur, secundo ad eius complementum ratio inducitur, ibi: *Sub arbore malo.* Circa primum sciendum quod in primitiva Ecclesia, Ecclesiae et eius ministris iniuriae multae inferebantur et opprobria, unde Maximianus Augustus Ecclesiam a Beato Marcello consecratam fecit stabulum publicum et Beatum Marcellum deputavit ad custodiam animalium, propter quod sponsa petit ab his et consimilibus per pacem Ecclesiae dandam liberari, dicens: *Quis mihi det te fratrem meum,* ratione humanitatis assumptae. *Suggentem ubera matris meae,* id est, Virginis Mariae, quae non solum dicitur mater Christi, sed etiam totius Ecclesiae. Quia autem hic locus intelligatur de Christo ad litteram, patet per translationem Chaldaicam apud Hebraeos autenticam quae sic habet: In illo tempore quo Rex Messias revelabit se Ecclesiae Israel, dicent ei filiae Israel, tu eris nobis ad fratrem. Sed Iudaei moderni expectant hoc futurum quod iam diu est praeteritum. *Ut inveniam te solum,* latria honoratum. Per hanc autem dictionem solum non excluditur Pater et Spiritus Sanctus, quia tres personae adorantur una adoratione quarum est una divinitas, sed per litteram solum excluditur idolorum servitus. *Foris,* id est, manifeste absque infidelium timore, quod postea fuit impletum tempore Constantini Imperatoris, qui concessit Ecclesias licite fabricari per totum imperium Romanum. Antea vero celebrabantur divina in cryptis martyrum et aliis locis occultis timore paganorum. *Et iam me nemo despiciat,* quia ante tempus Constantini multi contemptus fiebant Ecclesiae et eius ministris, ut dictum est, sed ipse lege ab eo promulgata prohibuit hoc fieri.

Apprehendam te, fidei devotione. *Et ducam,* id est, precibus meis faciam te venire per condescensionem bonitatis tuae. *In domum matris meae,* id est, in Ecclesiam Beatae Virgini consecratam, et etiam in consecratis aliis sanctis, quia totum cedit ad honorem Virginis cum in omnibus Ecclesiis honoretur. *Ibi me docebis,* revelando secreta mysteria Ecclesiae ministris, sicut patet in Beato Silvestro et multis aliis sanctis doctoribus et praelatis. *Et dabo tibi poculum ex vino condito,* id est, ex devotione fidelium quae placet Christo sicut vinum

the desire, then the reason for what complements it is brought out, beginning at the words *Under the apple tree* [ch. 8:5b]. Pertaining to the first of these sub-parts, it is necessary to know that, in the early Church, the Church and her ministers suffered many injustices and much hatred. For example, Maximianus Augustus turned a church, consecrated to St. Marcellus, into a public stable, and made Marcellus the stable boy. The bride sought to be free of these and similar shameful actions when God would grant peace to his Church. So she asks, *Who shall give thee to me for my brother,* a reference to Christ according to his human nature, *sucking the breasts of my mother,* that is, the Virgin Mary, who is called not only the mother of Christ, but also the mother of the whole Church. This passage refers literally to Christ, as is clear from the Chaldean translation, which the Hebrew scholars consider authentic. This text reads: "When the King, the Messiah, will reveal himself to the Church of Israel, the children of Israel will say to him, 'You will be to us a brother.'" Modern Jews expect this to happen in the future, though it already happened a long time ago. *That I may find thee alone,* given glory by means of worship. The word "alone" does not exclude the Father and the Holy Spirit, since all three persons who share the Godhead are adored as one. But the word "alone" does exclude the worship of idols. *Without,* that is, openly, without fear of unbelievers. This happened later, during the time of the emperor Constantine, who allowed churches to be built legally throughout the whole Roman Empire. It is a fact that, before [Constantine's time], worship services were held in the tombs of martyrs and in other secret places, for fear of the pagans. *And now no man may despise me.* Before Constantine's time there was a great deal of hatred for the Church and her ministers, as I just said, but when Constantine proclaimed this law, he stopped this activity.

[Ch. 8:2] *I will take hold of thee,* with devotion which arises from faith, *and bring [thee],* that is, by my prayers I will cause you to give in, out of your goodness, and come *into my mother's house,* that is, into the Church consecrated to the Blessed Virgin, and also into other consecrated holy places, because the Church concedes everything to the honor of the Virgin when she is honored in all churches. *There thou shalt teach me,* namely, when the Church reveals her secret mysteries to her ministers, as happened in the case of St. Sylvester, and in the case of many other holy doctors and prelates. *And I will give thee a cup of spiced wine,* that is, the devotion of the faithful which pleases Christ

bibentibus ipsum. *Et mustum malorum granatorum meorum.* Per *mustum* quod est vinum novum intelligitur devotio noviter conversorum, quod fuit impletum tempore Constantini, cuius exemplo multi valde devote receperunt baptismum.

Laeva eius, id est, sponsi. *Sub capite meo,* etc., quasi diceret, tunc ostendet mihi amicitiam sicut sponsus ad sponsam praedilectam. Et quia huius amicitiae continuatio est desideranda, et interruptio abhorrenda, ideo subditur:

Adiuro vos filiae Hierusalem, id est, personae de Ecclesia. *Ne suscitetis* etc., id est, quando sponsa obtinuerit quietem pacis quod non faciatis aliquid unde sponsus offendatur, et sponsae requies interrumpatur, ut sic prae admiratione prosperitatis suae dicatur:

Quae est ista quae ascendit de deserto, id est, de asperitate persecutionis tyrannorum. *Delitiis affluens,* tempore Constantini et aliorum principum Christianorum. Pax enim et tranquillitas post persecutiones magnas delitiae reputantur. Unde dicit Priscianus in minori volumine: Si quaeratur quid est summum bonum in vita, bene respondetur, pax; et Hester XIII: Ut absque ullo terrore vitam silentio transigentes, optata cunctis mortalibus pace fruerentur. *Innixa super dilectum suum,* quasi diceret, hanc tranquillitatem obtinuit, eo quod in Christo totaliter confidit.

Sub arbore, expresso sponsae desiderio. Hic consequenter ad eius impletionem allegatur ratio. Circa quod sciendum quod preces Ecclesiae sunt exaudibiles potissime per virtutem passionis Christi, ideo dicit sponsa: *Sub arbore malo,* id est, per virtutem sanctae crucis et tuae passionis. *Suscitavi te,* id est, invocavi te in oratione, ut cum in oratione dicit Ecclesia: Per crucem et passionem tuam libera nos Domine. Et sciendum quod littera malo non est hic adiectivum, ut credunt aliqui, exponentes hoc de arbore vetita Ade et Eve, quia in Hebraeo pro istis duabus dictionibus, arbore malo, ponitur punica,

just as wine pleases those who drink it, *and new wine of my pomegranates.* The word *mustum* [in the Latin], which means "new wine," refers to the devotion of the newly converted. This happened in Constantine's time when, following his example, many people were baptized in a display of great devotion.

[Ch. 8:3] *His left hand,* that is, the groom's left hand, *under my head [and his right hand shall embrace me],* meaning, God will show tenderness to me just as a groom shows tenderness to the bride whom he desires. Since it is desirable that this tenderness continues to be shown, and on the other hand it would be dreadful if it should cease, the text therefore adds,

[Ch. 8:4] *I adjure you, O daughters of Jerusalem,* that is, the people within the Church, *that you stir not up [nor awake my love till she please],* that is, when the bride shall have obtained her peace and quiet, you people within the Church must not do anything which might offend the groom and disturb the bride's rest, since everything is going so well for her.

[Ch. 8:5a] *Who is this that cometh up from the desert,* that is, from the bitterness of persecution by tyrants, *flowing with delights,* which happened under Constantine and other Christian rulers. For after great persecutions, people eagerly seek peace and tranquility. As Priscian says in one of his smaller books, "If you ask what is the highest good in life, the best answer is 'peace'." And Esther 13 [2] says: "I was not willing to abuse the greatness of my power, but rather to govern my subjects with mercy and leniency, that they might live quietly without any terror, and might enjoy peace, which all people desire." *Leaning upon her beloved,* meaning, the Church has obtained this tranquility by relying completely on Christ.

[Ch. 8:5b] *Under the [apple] tree.* With these words, the Church expresses her desire for her beloved, namely, Christ. Here the reason for the Church's satisfaction begins. Pertaining to this, you must first realize that the prayers of the Church are heard above all because of Christ's passion. Therefore, the bride says, *Under the apple tree,* that is, by virtue of your holy cross and passion, *I raised thee up,* that is, I called upon you in prayer, as when the Church prays, "By your cross and passion, free us, O Lord." You must also realize that the word "apple" here is not an adjective, as some think, explaining this as a reference to the tree which was forbidden to Adam and Eve, because in Hebrew, instead of two words "apple tree," there is only one word,

quae significat malogranatum, ideo expositio illa procedit ex igno-
rantia idiomatis Hebraei. Dicitur autem hic sancta crux malogranatum
quae est arbor fructifera, ad designandum fructum crucis qui est
innumerabilis. *Ibi corrupta est mater tua,* id est, synagoga quae dicitur
mater Dei ratione supradicta ca. III, quia in passione Christi
cessaverunt legalia tamquam mortificata. *Ibi violata est genitrix tua,*
repetitio est eiusdem ad maiorem assertionem. In Hebraeo habetur:
Ibi parturivit te mater tua, ibi parturivit te genetrix tua, et haec littera
veritati evangelicae est valde consona. Dicitur enim Ioh. XIX: Stabat
autem iuxta crucem mater eius etc., gladio doloris propter filium
transfixa, secundum quod praedixerat Sanctus Symeon, Luc. II: Et
tuam ipsius animam pertransibit gladius. Est igitur sensus: *Ibi,* id
est, iuxta crucem, *parturivit te mater tua,* id est, ut parturiens doluit
pro te, per talem modum loquendi dicit Apostolus, Gal. IIII: Filioli
mei quos iterum parturio donec formetur Christus in vobis. *Ibi
parturivit te genetrix tua.* Repetitio est eiusdem ad maiorem
expressionem. Et quia orationes Ecclesiae non solum sunt exaudibiles
per virtutem crucis, sed etiam per meritum Beatae Virginis, ideo
sponsa confidens de istis suffragiis petit a sponso.

Pone me ut signaculum super cor tuum, me perfecte diligendo,
quod enim valde diligitur super cor poni dicitur. *Ut signaculum super
brachium tuum,* me brachio tuae potentiae protegendo. *Quia fortis
est ut mors dilectio, dura sicut infernus aemulatio,* quasi diceret, licet
dilectio tua sit tam fortis in filiis Ecclesiae perfectis quod propter te
non timent poenam mortis, ut patet in martyribus, tamen *aemulatio,* id est, persecutio tyrannorum ex invidia et odio procedens
Christianorum, *Dura est sicut infernus* infirmis, propter quod indigent brachio protectionis tuae et beneficio pacis. *Lampades eius,* scilicet, tuae dilectionis in mentibus perfectorum. *Lampades ignis atque
flammarum,* id est, tam fortis est quod non potest obrui
persecutionibus tyrannorum, non sic autem est in infirmis, de quibus
subditur reddendo singula singulis.

"red," which refers to a pomegranate tree. The former explanation comes from ignorance of idiomatic Hebrew. Here Christ's holy cross is called a pomegranate tree, which yields a great deal of fruit, to signify the fruits of the cross, which are innumerable. *There thy mother was corrupted,* that is, the synagogue was corrupted. It is called the mother of God for the reason I gave earlier in chapter three. It is described as corrupted because, due to Christ's passion, its rights under the Law ceased as if they were dead. *There she was deflowered that bore thee.* This repeats the same thought to give it more emphasis. The Hebrew text has, *There your mother bore you. There your parent bore you.* This agrees particularly well with the truth of the Gospel. For it says in John 19 [25]: "Now there stood by the cross of Jesus his mother," pierced with a sword of sorrow because of her son, in accordance with what holy Simeon had prophesied in Luke 2 [53]: "And thy own soul a sword shall pierce." Therefore the sense of this verse is, *there,* that is, by the cross, *your mother bore you,* that is, bearing you caused her to suffer. In a similar way the Apostle says in Galatians 4 [19]: "My little children, of whom I am in labor again, until Christ be formed in you." *There your parent bore you.* This is a repetition of the same thought to make a deeper impression. And since the prayers of the Church are heard not only by virtue of the cross, but also by the merit of the Blessed Virgin, the bride therefore, confident that her petitions will be heard, makes a request of the groom:

[Ch. 8:6] *Put me as a seal upon thy heart,* by loving me perfectly, since what is loved above all else is said to be placed upon the heart, *as a seal upon thy arm,* by protecting me with your powerful arm. *For love is strong as death, jealousy as hard as hell,* meaning, though your love is felt so strongly by your Church's saints that, feeling your presence, they do not fear the punishment of death, as is clearly seen in the case of the martyrs, nevertheless, *jealousy,* that is, tyrannical persecution which comes from envy and hatred of Christians, *is as hard as hell* for the weak [in faith], which is why they need your protecting arm and the blessing of peace which you grant them. *His lamps,* that is, a sense of your love in the minds of the saints. *The lamps thereof are fire and flames,* that is, so strongly is your love felt that it cannot be destroyed by the persecutions of tyrants. However, your love is not felt so strongly by the weak [in faith], about whom the text adds, letting a single person stand for many individuals.

Si dederit homo omnem substantiam domus suae pro dilectione, divina. *Quasi nihil despiciet eam,* quasi diceret, pro amore tuo contemnere bona exteriora etiam possunt infirmi, et supplendum est, non sic autem propriam vitam martyrium sustinendo. Et est hic modus loquendi apud Hebraeos qui dicitur decurtatus, ubi oportet aliquid supplere ad habendum intellectum, sicut II Reg. V, proposuerat David praemium ei qui percussisset Iebusaeum etc., et supplendum est quod illud praemium erat quod fieret magister militiae, ut exprimitur I Parali. X [XI]: Qui percusserit Iebusaeum in primis erit princeps et dux. De hac autem infirmitate ad martyrium, et promptitudine ad dimissionem temporalium, dicit Greg., Omel. XXXIIII: Fortasse laboriosum non est homini relinquere sua, sed valde laboriosum est relinquere semetipsum; minus quippe est abnegare quod habet, valde enim multum est abnegare quod est. Est igitur sententia in hac parte quod sponsa petit temporalem pacem, qua etsi non indigent perfecti quibus lucrum esset pro Christo mori, tamen ea indigent imperfecti quorum multo maior est numerus in Ecclesia Dei.

Soror nostra. Hic consequenter ponitur adimpletio desiderii sponsae in pacis largitione. Et dividitur in tres partes, quia primo ponitur pacis largitio, secundo Ecclesiae pacificatae ampliatio, ibi: *Vinea fuit,* tertio finalis conclusio, ibi: *Quae habitas.* Circa primum dicitur in persona sponsi sibi compatientis: *Soror nostra,* id est, Ecclesia quae dicitur soror Christi eadem ratione qua Christus dicitur eius frater in principio huius ca. *Parvula,* id est, humilis et abiecta inter homines huius saeculi, et hoc fuit usque ad tempus Constantini. *Et ubera non habet,* id est, libertatem effundendi lac sacrae doctrinae per fidei Catholicae praedicationem, quam tunc Ecclesia non audebat publice praedicare, sed tantum in occulto docere exceptis aliquibus perfectis qui pro praedicatione fidei ultro se offerebant morti. *Quid faciemus.* Per hoc intelligitur Pater et Spiritus Sanctus operari cum Filio. Opera enim Trinitatis sunt indivisa. *Sorori nostrae in die quando*

[Ch. 8:7] *If a man should give all the substance of his house for love,* that is, to obtain God's love, *he shall despise it as nothing,* meaning, to obtain God's love the weak are willing to spurn all external goodness except—here one has to supply the missing phrase—what is truly good, martyrdom. This is the way the Hebrews speak, not completing their sentences, so that it is necessary to supply something in order to understand them. For example, according to 2 Kings 5 [8], David had offered a prize to the one who would strike the Jebusites, but one must supply the fact that the prize was that this person should become the leader of the army, as we learn from 1 Paralipomenon [1 Chronicles] 10 [ch.11:6]: "Whosoever shall first strike the Jebusites shall be the head and chief captain." Besides this, pertaining to weakness in the face of martyrdom, and swiftness to give up temporal possessions, Gregory says in Homily 34: "Perhaps it is not difficult for a man to give up his possessions, but it is very difficult to give up himself. Indeed, it is a small thing to deny what one has, but it is a big thing to deny what one is." The thought of this section, then, is that the bride seeks temporal peace, which, even if the saints (for whom it is gain to die for Christ) do not need it, nevertheless the weak [in faith] (which are a much larger number in the Church of God) do need it.

[Ch. 8:8] *Our sister.* Next comes the fulfillment of the bride's desire when peace is bestowed on her. It is divided into three parts. First there is the bestowal of peace. Second, the growth of the Church in the time of this peace, beginning at the words, *[the peaceable] had a vineyard* [ch. 8:11]. Third, the conclusion, at the words, *Thou that dwellest* [ch. 8:13]. Pertaining to the first, the groom, who is filled with sorrow, says, *Our sister,* that is, the Church, which is called the sister of Christ for the same reason that Christ is called her brother at the beginning of this chapter, *is little,* that is, humble and despised by the people of this present age, which was the case up to the time of Constantine, *and hath no breasts,* that is, the Church did not have the freedom to pour out the milk of sacred doctrine through the preaching of the Catholic faith, which the Church did not dare to preach publicly at that time, but only in secret, except for some saints who offered themselves voluntarily to be killed for preaching the faith. *What shall we do?* By "we" the Father and the Holy Spirit are understood to be working with the Son. For the activities of the Trinity are indivisible. *[What shall we do] to our sister in the day when she is to be*

alloquenda est, id est, a principibus advocanda est, sicut patet de Constantino qui Beatum Silvestrum Papam cum clero suo advocavit ut per eum consequeretur corporis et animae sanitatem, et simile fecerunt eius exemplo multi principes et potentes per orbem terrarum.

Si murus est, accipitur hic si pro quia, quasi diceret, quia murus est fortis contra persecutiones et hoc ratione perfectorum, quorum meritis subveniendum est imperfactis, ideo subditur: *Aedificemus super eum propugnacula argentea,* id est, adiungamus ei per susceptionem fidei principes ad defensionem infirmorum. In Hebraeo habetur: *Aedificemus super eum palatium argenteum,* per quod idem designatur quod per propugnacula quia per palatium etiam secundum communem modum loquendi intelligitur regalis potentia. Et dicitur argenteum, quia Constantinus et alii principes in promotione Ecclesiae multum expenderunt argentum. *Si ostium est,* id est, quia Ecclesia est ostium per quod ingreditur ad caelestae regnum. *Compingamus illud,* id est, fortificemus. *Tabulis cedrinis,* id est, doctoribus sacris qui dicuntur cedri propter scientiae et vitae eminentiam et fidei integritatem, sicut cedrus est arbor valde alta et a vermibus non perforatur. Aliter potest etiam exponi: *Si murus est* etc., id est, quia usque nunc Ecclesia fuit parva et depressa. Elevemus eam, ad statum honorificum et magnum, et quia Ecclesia de huiusmodi beneficiis fuit grata, ideo subditur in eius persona:

Ego murus, propugnaculis munitus per potentiam principum, tamen ex dono Christi principaliter. *Et ubera mea sicut turris,* sicut praedictum est per ubera sponsae intelligitur lactis copia sacrae doctrinae quae abundavit a conversione Constantini, quia ex tunc Ecclesia habuit libertatem publice praedicandi et docendi, et quia haec doctrina non solum est ad informationem morum, sed etiam ad confutationem infidelium et hereticorum, ideo subditur: *Sicut turris,* de qua dicit Magister Sententiarum: Fidem nostram Daviticae turris clypeis munire vel potius munitam ostendere studuimus; sicut supra allegatum est de doctoribus Veteris Testamenti, ca. IIII. *Ex quo facta sum coram eo quasi pacem reperiens,* scilicet, ex

spoken to?, that is, when the Church is called upon for help by princes. This happened when Constantine, through his priest, called upon St. Sylvester the Pope, so that, through him, Constantine might gain health for his body and soul. Following Constantine's example, many princes and rulers throughout the world did a similar thing.

[Ch. 8:9] *If she be a wall.* Here "if" means "because," as if the text said, Because she, the Church, is a wall, she stands firm against persecutions. And since the merits of the martyrs aid those who are weak in their faith, the text therefore adds, *let us build upon it bulwarks of silver,* that is, let us add to the Church princes who have come to faith, that they might defend the weak. The Hebrew has, *Let us build upon it a palace of silver.* "Palace" signifies the same thing as "bulwarks," because a palace commonly indicates royal power. The palace is described as "silver" because Constantine and other princes spent a great deal of silver to advance the Church's interests. *If she be a door,* that is, because the Church is the door through which one enters the kingdom of heaven, *let us join it together,* that is, we will fortify her *with boards of cedar,* that is, with holy teachers. They are called "cedar" because of the eminence of their knowledge and life, and the soundness of their faith, just as a cedar is a tall and stately tree, and worms do not eat through it. The text may also be explained this way: *If she be a wall* etc., that is, because the Church up to Constantine's time was small and compressed, therefore let us lift her up to a great and honorable position. And because the Church was favored with these blessings, therefore, as if the Church herself were speaking, the text adds:

[Ch. 8:10] *I am a wall,* fortified with bulwarks by the power of princes; however, I am above all fortified by the gift of Christ, *and my breasts are as a tower.* As I explained before, the bride's breasts mean the abundance of the milk of sacred doctrine, which became abundant from the conversion of Constantine onward, because from that time forth the Church has had the freedom to preach and teach publicly. And since this teaching is not only useful for improving morals, but also for confuting the faithless and heretics, the text therefore adds, *as a tower.* Pertaining to this the Master of the Sentences says: "Let us endeavor to fortify our faith with the shield of the tower of David, or rather, let us endeavor to show that our faith is thus fortified," as he said about the teachers of the Old Testament which I mentioned already in chapter four. *Since I am become in his presence*

tempore Constantini qui tertia die sui baptismi legem promulgavit, ut quicumque iniuriam faceret Christiano, bonorum suorum mediam amitteret facultatem.

Vinea. Hic consequenter ponitur Ecclesiae pacem habentis ampliatio, et primo quantam ad multiplicationem credentium cum dicitur: *Vinea,* id est, Ecclesia, ut supra dictum est ca. VII. *Fuit pacifico,* id est, Christo qui per sanguinem suum omnia pacificavit quae in caelis sunt et in terris, Col. I. *In ea,* scilicet, urbe *quae habet populos,* id est, Roma, in qua habitabant aliqui de omnibus terrae populis, vel quia omnes populi Romano imperio cuius caput est Roma erant subiecti, unde dicit Leo Papa in sermone apostolorum Petri et Pauli: Dispositioni divini operis maxime congruebat ut multa regna uno confederarentur imperio, et cito pervios haberet populos praedicatio generalis quos unius tenebat regimen civitatis. *Tradidit eam custodibus,* id est, Beato Petro et eius successoribus. *Vir affert pro fructu eius mille argenteos.* Vir ille intelligitur Constantinus qui fuit virtuosus contra hostes imperii Romani de quibus triumphavit, et contra hostes generis humani, scilicet, demones quos per fidem superavit, et ipse, *Pro fructu* vineae, id est, pro fructu Ecclesiae multas et magnas fecit expensas quae per mille argenteos hic designantur. Vel potest dici quod hic ponitur singulare pro plurali, scilicet, mille pro multis milibus sicut Exo. VIII: Venit musca gravissima, id est, multitudo muscarum.

Vinea mea coram me est, mutatur hic modus loquendi a tertia persona ad primam de Domino huius vineae qui est ipse Christus, de quo dictum fuerat in tertia persona: *Tradidit eam custodibus.* Et ne credatur quod per hanc traditionem dimiserit Ecclesiae custodiam, ideo dicit: *Vinea mea coram me est,* id est, ad eius custodiam praesentialiter et principaliter assisto, propter quod dicitur in Ps. CXXVI: Nisi Dominus custodierit civitatem etc., propter quod de hac custodia multo maiores gratiae debentur Christo quam praelatis Ecclesiae, ideo subdit sponsa: *Mille tui pacifici* etc., tui pacifici sunt genitivi casus singularis numeri, quod patet per litteram Hebraicam

as one finding peace, that is, [I, the Church, have found peace] since the time of Constantine, who on the third day after his baptism, promulgated the law that whoever should cause harm to a Christian would lose most of his possessions.

[Ch. 8:11] *A vineyard.* Next comes the growth of the Church once it was at peace, first in terms of more believers. *A vineyard,* that is, the Church, as I explained above in chapter seven, *the peaceable had,* that is, Christ by shedding his blood brought peace to all things in heaven and on earth, as it says in Colossians 1 [20]. *In that,* that is, that particular city, *which hath people.* This is a reference to Rome where people from all over the world were living, or perhaps because all people were subject to the Roman Empire which had its head-quarters in Rome. As Pope Leo says in a sermon on the apostles Peter and Paul: "God arranged it so that many kingdoms were united under the rule of one city, and thus a general proclamation could quickly reach all the various people whom the government of that one city controlled." *He let out the same to keepers,* that is, to St. Peter and his successors. *A man bringeth for the fruit thereof a thousand pieces of silver.* This is a reference to Constantine, who displayed courage against the enemies of the Roman Empire whom he defeated, and against the enemies of the human race, namely, the demons whom he over-came by faith. That same Constantine, *for the fruit* of the vineyard, that is, for the benefit of the Church, incurred many heavy expenses which are signified here by a thousand pieces of silver. Or one could say that here the singular is used for the plural, that is, a thousand for many thousands, as in Exodus 8 [24] which says: "And there came a very grievous fly," that is, a swarm of flies.

[Ch. 8:12] *My vineyard is before me.* The sentence style is changed here from the use of the third person to the first person. The speaker here is the Lord of this vineyard, who is actually Christ. *He let out the same to keepers.* One must not suppose that by this "letting out to keepers" Christ would give up his protection of the Church. There-fore he says, *My vineyard is before me,* that is, I am personally taking care of my Church, more so than anyone else, as it says in Psalm 126 [1]: "Unless the Lord keep the city, [he watcheth in vain that keepeth it]." Therefore the Church owes much greater thanks to Christ for his protection than to the Church's prelates. With this in mind the bride adds, *A thousand are of thee, the peaceable, [and two hundred for them that keep the fruit thereof].* "Of thee, the peaceable" is in the

quae talis est: *Mille tibi pacifico,* et est sensus quod sicut mille est maior numerus quam ducenti, sic maiores gratiae debentur Christo qui pacificus hic dicitur de conservatione Ecclesiae quam praelatis qui sub eo custodes sunt huius vineae, et honor exhibendus praelatis convenienter intelligitur per ducentenarium, secundum illud Apostoli, I Timot. V: Qui bene praesunt presbyteri duplici honore digni habeantur. Inferioribus autem simplex centenarius promittitur reddendus Math. XIX: Centuplum accipiet.

Quae habitas. Hic ultimo ponitur finalis conclusio quae stat in hoc quod Ecclesia de praesenti miseria tollatur et ad caelestem gloriam transferatur, quod fit partialiter in praesenti quantum ad sanctos qui ad gloriam assumuntur, sed generaliter fiet peracto iudicio finali cum Christus tradiderit regum Deo et Patri, I Cor. XV. Ad hoc igitur desiderandum et petendum sponsus inducit sponsam dicens: *Quae habitas in hortis,* id est, in ecclesiis per orbem dispersis quae dicuntur horti, quia in eis fideles sunt plantati, et quia ad litteram frequenter arbores circa ecclesias sunt plantatae. *Amici auscultant* te, id est, angeli ad quorum consortium fideles tui sunt transferendi et de tua salute solliciti, desiderant audire tuas orationes devotas, ideo subditur: *Fac me audire vocem tuam,* id est, tui desiderii expressionem in oratione devota, quam consequenter profert sponsa dicens:

Fuge dilecte mi. Per hanc fugam non intelligitur recessus dilecti ab ea cum dixerit supra ca. praecedenti: *Ego dilecto meo et ad me conversio eius,* per mutuam inhaesionem inseperabilem, secundum illud Apostoli Ro. VIII: Quis nos separabit a caritate quae est in Christo Ihesu etc., sed per eam intelligitur velox translatio sponsae cum sponso ad caelestia, quod summe desiderat et petit in orationibus suis Ecclesia, ut patet in officio ecclesiastico, et per talem modum exponit hanc fugam Rabbi Salomon trahendo tamen litteram ad errorem Iudaicum, dicens quod plebs Iudaica per hoc petit liberari a captivitate ista in qua est modo per Messiam futurum. Sed haec expositio fundatur super falsum fundamentum, ideo bene exponitur

genitive singular [in Latin]. However, the Hebrew text actually says, *A thousand for thee, O peaceable one.* The sense is that just as a thousand is greater than two hundred, so greater thanks are owed to Christ, "the peaceable one," who takes care of his Church, than to prelates who are caretakers of this vineyard under him. The honor that should be shown to prelates is fittingly understood by "two hundred," in accordance with what the Apostle says in 1 Timothy 5 [17]: "Let the priests that rule well be esteemed worthy of double honor." A single "hundred" is enough for lesser individuals, as Matthew 19 [29] says: "He shall receive a hundredfold."

[Ch. 8:13] *Thou that dwellest.* We come at last to the conclusion, the deliverance of the Church from her present sufferings and her reception into heavenly glory. This occurs in part in this present age when saints are taken up into glory. But it will occur in general at the final judgment when Christ hands over the kingdom to God the Father, 1 Corinthians 15 [24]. The groom therefore leads his bride toward this highly desired end, saying, *Thou that dwellest in the gardens,* that is, you who dwell in the churches spread throughout the world, called "gardens" because the faithful are planted in them, and because quite often trees are literally planted around churches. *The friends harken* to you, that is, the angels, into whose care Christians are given, and who are concerned about their salvation. They desire to hear the devout prayers of Christians. Therefore the text adds, *Make me hear thy voice,* that is, let me hear what you desire in a devoutly offered prayer. The bride then offers this kind of prayer, saying:

[Ch. 8:14] *Flee away, O my beloved.* This "flee away" does not mean a lessening of the desire which the bride showed when she said in the preceding chapter, *I to my beloved, and his turning is toward me* [ch. 7:10], in a mutual and inseparable union, in accordance with what the Apostle says in Romans 8 [35, 39]: "Who then shall separate us from the love which is in Christ Jesus." But rather this "flee away" means the taking of the bride with the groom to heaven in the near future, which the Church so highly desires and seeks in her prayers, as is clearly seen in the Church's liturgy. Rabbi Solomon, however, explains "flee away" in line with mistaken Jewish belief, saying that with these words the Jewish people seek to be freed from the captivity in which they now live by the coming of the Messiah. But this explanation is based on a shaky foundation. These words are

modo praedicto ut sit sensus: *Fuge dilecte mi,* id est, educ me tecum de miseria praesentis saeculi. *Et assimilare capreae* etc., id est, fac istud velociter. *Super montes aromatum,* id est, transferendo me tecum ad caelos qui dicuntur montes, Ps. CXX: Levavi oculos meos in montes etc., qui dicuntur hic *montes aromatum* quia ibi est suavissima requies electorum. Ad quam nos perducat qui cum Patre et Spiritu Sancto vivet et regnat in saecula saeculorum. Amen.

Postilla venerabilis fratris
Nicolai de Lyra super Cantica Canticorum finit.

better explained as I did. So once again the meaning is, *Flee away, O my beloved,* that is, take me to be with you, away from the miseries of this present age, *and be like to the roe [and to the young hart],* that is, do this quickly, *upon the mountains of aromatical spices,* that is, by lifting me up with you into the heavens which are referred to as mountains, as in Psalm 120 [1]: "I have lifted up my eyes to the mountains [from whence help shall come to me]." The heavens are here called "mountains of aromatical spices" because there there is the sweetest rest for the elect. To this place may he take us, he who lives and reigns with the Father and the Holy Spirit, forever and ever. Amen.

The end of the *Postilla* of the venerable brother, Nicholas of Lyra, on the Song of Songs.

APPENDIX
Cantica

From *Biblia cum postillis*. Vol. 2, fol. 132r.
Venice: Franciscus Renner, 1482.

¶ Postilla venerabilis fratris Nicolai de lyra super Cantica incipit. Cap.j.

a

Sculetur me ꝛc. Expedito primo Salomonis libro in quo traduntur documenta que faciunt ad illustrationem mentis. ꞇ secundo in quo inducimur ad contemptū affluentie mobilis. hic consequenter incipit terti⁹ inducens ad amorem superne felicitatis. sicut dictū fuit plenius in principio primi libri. vbi posui quandam prefationē pro istis tribus libris. Appetitus ꝓo felicitatis superne procedit ex amore mutuo dei ꞇ rationalis creature. qui in hoc libro describitur ꝯ ut plenius videbitur prosequēdo. tamen ad maiorem dicendorum intelligentiam aliqua sunt hic premittēda. Primū est ꝙ translatio nostra in pluribus locis discrepat a littera hebraica. ꞇ similiter signatio capituloꝝ. Secundum est ꝙ totus iste liber ꝓcedit parabolice. nec tamen apparet lucide quibus personis determinate parabole ꝯm sensum litteralem sint applicande. ꞇ hoc cum predictis difficultatē ingerit in hoc libro. Si enim hoc appareret sicut Judic.ix. vbi dicitur: Dixerunt autē omnia ligna ad rhamnū. veni ꞇ impera super nos. ex irā sequēte manifeste patet ꝙ intelligitur de sichimitis ꞇ abimelech quē vnxerunt super se regem. tunc facile esset hunc librū exponere. sed hoc non apparet nisi in quodā generali. f. ꝙ iste liber loquatur parabolice de amore mutuo sponsi ꞇ sponse. sed quis sit iste sponsus ꞇ que sit b sponsa clare nō apparet ex irā. ꝓpter quod accipiunt varie a diuersis. Quidam enim dixerunt ꝙ hic accipitur sponsus ad litteram ipse salomon. ꞇ sponsa filia pharaonis vxor eius predilecta. sed hoc non videt verū. qꝛ lz hic amor inter sponsum ꞇ sponsam potuerit esse licitus. utpote infra limites matrimonij ꝯtentus. sicut dixi plenius super tertiū librum Reg.iij.ca. tamen carnalis fuit. ꞇ frequenter habet talis amor aliquid inhonestum ꞇ illicitum adiunctū. ꝓpter quod descriptio talis amoris non videtur ad libros sacre scripture canonicos pertinere. maxime qꝛ huiusmodi libri spiritu sancto dictante sunt scripti. Salomon autem amorem sui ad vxore ꞇ econuerso. ꞇ delectamenta ad b sequentia cognouit per experientiā ꞇ non per sancti spiritus reuelatiōe. ꝓpter quod hic liber qui semper fuit ab hebreis ꞇ latinis inter canonicos libros reputatus. ut patet per hiero. in ꝓlogo galeato. non videtur de hoc amore conscriptus. Propter quod hebrei dicunt ꝙ iste liber loquitur parabolice de amore dei ꞇ plebis iudaice. quam sibi desponsauit in legis datione Exo.xx.

From *Biblia cum postillis*. Vol. 2, fol. 132r, col. 1.

electum qui in fine mundi nasciturus e̅ quot sanctos protulit quasi tot palmites misit. Ecclesia vo sic accepta respicit diuersa tempora. ⁊ in aliquibus offendit sponsum. ⁊ in alijs placauit. Item constituta est ex diuersis gentibus. s. ex iudeis ⁊ gentibus. ex iustis ⁊ peccatoribus. ex prelatis ⁊ subditi͡. ⁊ hec ⁊ p͡similia faciu̅t. difficultate̅ in hoc

C Incipiunt Cantica canticorum Cap. I

Osculetur ᵃ me osculo oris sui. Quia ᵇ melio ra su̅t vbera tua vino: fragrantia ᶜ vnguentis ᵈ opti mis. Oleum ᵉ effusum nomen tuum: ideo ᶠ adolescentule di lexerunt tc. Trahe ᵍ me post tc. Currem ᵍᵇ in ʰ odore vnguetoꝝ

libro. quia frequenter fit transitus de vno tempore ad aliud. ⁊ de vna parte ecclesie ad aliam. . ⁊ de ecclesia ad deum ⁊ ecouer so quasi sub eodem conte ptu lr̅e. ⁊ hoc apter cone xionem sponsi ⁊ sponse ad inuicem ⁊ partium eccle sie in vnam fide̅. sicut ple ni⁹ dixi in pncipio Ben. in regulis de itellectu sa cre scripture. Sciendum autem q̅ l3 ecclesia a pn cipio mundi inceperit. ut predictum est. tamen spe cialiter nomen sponse pri

mo in oatione legis in monte synai accepit. per quam plebs ísi l̅ fuit desponsata deo per fidem ⁊ latriam. alijs gentibus ad idolatriam de clinantibus. apter quod salomon spiritu sancto dictante describen do amorem dei ⁊ ecclesie sub noibus sponsi ⁊ sponse. incepit a tempo re egressus de egyptiaca seruitute. quia tu̅c ler fuit data. Igitur iste liber diuiditur in duas partes. ⁊ in prima describitur amor iste pro tempore veteris testamenti. ⁊ in secunda pro tempore noui. secu̅da in cipit. ʃ. ca. vij. Prima diuiditur in tres. q̅ primo describitur amor predictus put respicit egressum de terra egypti. secundo pgressum p viam deserti. ibi: Dum esset rex. tertio ingressu̅ termini. s. iudee. iiij. ca. ibi: Adam. Prima in duas. quia p ponitur amoroſ͡ sponse peti tio. 2° gratiosa sponsi rñsio. ibi: Si ignoras Prima adhuc in duas. quia p ponit petitio amoris. 2° exclusio errons. ibi: Nigra sum. Cir ca primum sciendum q̅ populus israel qui spose nomine hic intelligi tur multum desiderauit de egypto exire. ut liber a seruitute dura pos set deo liberius seruire. ⁊ ei amore feruentius inherere. ut habet Exo.

From *Biblia cum postillis*. Vol. 2, fol. 132r, col. 2.